Also by Shashi Tharoor

Nonfiction

*Reasons of State*
*India: From Midnight to the Millennium*
*Kerala: God's Own Country* (with M. F. Husain)
*Nehru: The Invention of India*

Fiction

*The Five-Dollar Smile and Other Stories*
*The Great Indian Novel*
*Show Business*
*Riot*

Bookless
in
Baghdad

# Bookless in Baghdad

## REFLECTIONS ON WRITING AND WRITERS

Shashi Tharoor

Arcade Publishing New York

# For Cat
## ma belle dame sans merci

FIRST EDITION

The essays collected in this book have appeared, in slightly different form, in the following publications: the *New York Times*, *New York Times Book Review*, *Washington Post*, *Washington Post Book World*, *Indian Express*, *Hindu*, *Seminar*, *India Today Plus*, *World Policy Journal*, *International Herald Tribune*, and *Newsweek International*. They have been revised, updated, and edited for inclusion in this volume. Permission to reproduce previously published material is gratefully acknowledged.

Though the author is a senior official of the United Nations, none of the opinions expressed in this book are to be construed as those of the organization or of the author in his official capacity.

*Library of Congress Cataloging-in-Publication Data*

    Tharoor, Shashi, 1956–
       Bookless in Baghdad : reflections on writing and writers / by Shashi Tharoor. —1st ed.
       p. cm.
       ISBN 1-55970-757-7
    1. Tharoor, Shashi, 1956– 2. Authors, Indic—20th century—Biography. 3. Tharoor, Shashi, 1956– —Books and reading. 4. Books and reading—Iraq—Baghdad. 5. Literature—History and criticism. 6. Books and reading. 7. Authorship. I. Title.

    PR9499.3.T535Z465 2005
    823'.914—dc22                            2004023457

Published in the United States by Arcade Publishing, Inc., New York
Distributed by Time Warner Book Group

10  9  8  7  6  5  4  3  2  1

Designed by API

EB

PRINTED IN THE UNITED STATES OF AMERICA

# Contents

FIVE: INTERROGATIONS

# Preface

OVER THE YEARS I HAVE FOUND MYSELF expressing opinions on a host of subjects, in the op-ed pages of an assortment of newspapers around the world and as a fortnightly columnist, initially for the *Indian Express* and, since April 2001, for the *Hindu*. My pieces have ranged eclectically from cricket to politics and from Indian history to the challenges facing the United Nations. And many of them, inevitably, have dealt with matters literary.

*Bookless in Baghdad* is a collection of forty of my essays on literary topics, which have appeared in a variety of publications over the past decade. They span a broad range of concerns emerging from my own experience as an Indian writer (and reader!), but they share a literary provenance: none of my writings on nonliterary subjects have been included. All the essays have been written for the layperson rather than the academic specialist. They vary in length and tone depending on the publication for which they were first written, and though many have been revised and updated to see the light of day in 2005, I have not altered the views or judgments they originally contained.

Though I have reviewed many books, including several Indian novels, I have not included any of my book reviews in this collection. Rather, this volume seeks to assemble my ruminations on aspects of the literary experience that go beyond any single book. I hope that these essays will prove illuminating at times and provocative at others, and above all that they will impart something of the pleasure that the acts of reading and writing have always given me. To me, books are like the toddy tapper's hatchet, striking through the rough husk that enshrouds our minds to tap into the exhilaration that ferments within.

More than a century ago, Walter Pater wrote of art as "professing frankly to give nothing but the highest quality to your moments as they pass." That may be all that reading offers; but it is no modest aspiration.

# I

## Inspirations

# 1

# Growing Up with Books in India

GROWING UP AS THE CHILD of middle-class parents in urban India in the late 1950s and '60s meant growing up with books. Television did not exist in the Bombay of my boyhood, and Nintendo (let alone the personal computer) was not even a gleam in an inventor's eye. If your siblings were, as in my case, four and six years younger (and worse, female), there was only one thing to do when you weren't with your friends. Read.

I read copiously, rapidly, and indiscriminately. Chronic asthma often confined me to bed, but I found so much pleasure in the books piled up by my bedside that I stopped resenting my illness. Soon reading became the central focus of my existence; there was not a day in my childhood that did not feature a book, or several. One year I kept a list of the volumes I'd finished (comics didn't count), hoping to reach 365 before the calendar did. I made it before Christmas.

An abiding memory is of my mother coming into my room around eleven every night and switching off the light.

I wasn't smart enough to think of holding a flashlight under the covers, but sometimes I would wait for my parents to fall asleep in their room, then surreptitiously switch my light on again to finish the book they'd interrupted.

It was, of course, my mother who'd started me off on the bad habit to begin with. When I was still in diapers, she would read to me from the Noddy books of Enid Blyton, stories about a nodding wooden doll and his friends in Toyland. My mother jokes that she read them so badly, I couldn't wait to grab the books from her myself; by the time I was three I was reading Noddy, and soon moving on to other stories by Blyton, easily the world's most prolific children's author, whose prodigious output (over two hundred books) could take you through an entire childhood. When I outgrew Noddy, there were Enid Blyton fairy tales, nursery fantasies, and retold legends; by seven I started on her thrilling mysteries of the Five-Find-Outers (and Dog); by eight I discovered her tales of British boarding-school life, midnight feasts and all; by nine I was launched on the adventures of the "Famous Five" and of four intrepid British teenagers in another series that always had the word *adventure* in its titles (*The Ship of Adventure*, *The Castle of Adventure*, and so on). Today, Enid Blyton has become the target of well-intentioned but overearnest revisionists, her stories assailed for racism, sexism, and overall political incorrectness. But my postcolonial generation (and today's Indians too) read her books entranced by her extraordinary storytelling skills and quite indulgent of her stereotypes. After two hundred years of the Raj, Indian children know instinctively how to filter the foreign — to appreciate the best in things British, and not to take the rest seriously.

For colonialism gave us a literature that did not spring from our own environment, and whose characters, concerns, and situations bore no relation to our own lives. This didn't bother us in the slightest: a Bombay child read Blyton the same way a Calcutta kindergartner sang "Jingle Bells" without ever having seen snow or sleigh. If the stories were alien, we weren't alienated; they were to be read and enjoyed, not mined for relevance.

Indeed, the most popular British children's books other than Enid Blyton's were the ones that didn't take themselves too seriously. My own favorites were the "William" books of Richmal Crompton, minor masterpieces of brilliantly plotted hilarity involving the escapades of an irrepressible schoolboy (all tousled hair, grubby face, and cheeks bulging with licorice allsorts) who was forever tumbling into ditches, pulling off outrageous schemes, and messing up his elder sister's love life. A close second came the Billy Bunter series by Frank Richards, whose stories under half a dozen pseudonyms earned him attention in George Orwell's famous essay on schoolboy fiction. Richards created an uproarious world of British public-school characters, from the eponymous Bunter ("a fat, frabjous frump") to his doughty Yorkshire classmate John Bull. There was even a dusky Indian princeling, improbably named Hurree Jamset Ram Singh, who played cricket magnificently, mixed his metaphors in a series of sage howlers, and answered to the name of "Inky." I suppose that, reading the books in independent India half a century after they were written, I ought to have been offended; but I was merely amused, for Frank Richards never wrote a dull word in his long and productive career.

Another hardy perennial was Capt. W. E. Johns, whose hero Biggles made his literary debut as a World War I flying ace and agelessly fought through World War II and the Cold War before his creator finally — in the RAF jargon he made so familiar to us — "went West." (Biggles's adventures inspired my own first work of published fiction at age ten — a credulity-stretching saga of an Anglo-Indian fighter pilot, "Operation Bellows" — but that is another story.)

Blyton, Bunter, Biggles: that insidious imperialist Macaulay had done his work too well, his policies spawning a breed of Indians the language of whose education made them a captive market for the British imagination. What about Indian books? Sadly, I suffered a major handicap: my parents' peripatetic life (I was born in London, grew up in Bombay, and would move to Calcutta before I turned thirteen) cut me off from the literature of my mother tongue, Malayalam. As with other children of migratory Indians, English became the language not only of my schoolbooks but of my private life: I played with my friends in English, quarreled with my sisters in English, wrote to my relatives in English — and read for pleasure in English.

The colonial inheritance made this a common predicament among urban, English-educated Indians. But where more proficiently bilingual children like my former wife, growing up in Calcutta, also read nonsense verse and fairy tales in vivid Bengali, I had to make do with Lear and Grimm and Hans Christian Andersen in English. There were few good Indian children's books available in English in a market still dominated by the British. The one area where Indian publishers could hold their own was in retelling the Indian classics. I remember several versions of the traditional tales I'd heard from my grandmother — episodes from the Ramayana and the Mahabharata (which later inspired my first novel), and the fables of the ancient Jatakas and the Panchatantra. Many of the fables had become familiar in the West through their retelling by Aesop, and thanks to the colonial legacy, we had the European versions too.

The other Indian stories I remember enjoying as a child were clever short tales about Birbal and Tenaliraman, two wise and witty men from opposite corners of the country who resolved problems in what were essentially extended anecdotes. The government-sponsored Children's Book Trust began publishing subsidized books for Indian children during the 1960s, but their quality was erratic and could not match the allure of their imported competitors. Today, their list features Indian equivalents of Enid Blyton, including a series devised explicitly to counter gender stereotypes. Indian kids today also have an indigenous answer to America's famous Classics Illustrated, the Amar Chitra Katha series, which retells myths, legends, and historical stories in attractive comics — and has Indianized the sensibilities of its readers in a manner unavailable to me when I was growing up in India.

But English did give me access to a broader world. Before I was thirteen I had read English translations, and competent abridgments, of Camus, Chekhov, Dostoyevsky, Hermann Hesse, and Tolstoy. Mark Twain and Melville's

*Moby-Dick*, also adapted for younger readers, brought America to us, but in our daily reading the United States didn't fare as well as the former colonial power. Of course we had access to the Bobbsey Twins and the Hardy Boys, but there seemed to be something faintly brash and spurious about them: British books, we were brought up to believe, set the real standard.

The classroom, with its British-inspired curriculum, was a rich source of inspiration. At the age of nine I was reading Lamb's *Tales from Shakespeare*, at ten Charles Dickens's *Oliver Twist* (both unabridged); and the Bard himself, mildly expurgated, made an appearance on the syllabus when I was eleven. In the same year, an otherwise detestable teacher dictated a passage from P. G. Wodehouse as a spelling test, and launched me on the first great passion of my life.

It took me some seven years to find and finish all ninety-five of the master's books, but the pleasure he gave will last a lifetime. When, a month short of my twelfth birthday, my father — then thirty-eight — was taken to the hospital after a massive heart attack, the only thing that could console me, keep me whole and sane, as my father battled for his life in intensive care, was the compelling magic of a Wodehouse novel. To be transported to his idyllic world of erudite butlers and eccentric baronets, with its overfed pigs, bellowing aunts, and harebrained attempts to pinch policemen's helmets, offered what every stressed-out child needs, an alternative to reality. (Wodehouse's farcically elaborate plotting, drolly literate style, and sidesplitting humor were, of course, their own rewards.) Dad pulled through, and I have remained eternally grateful. India is still the only country where Wodehouse has both a mass and a cult following, if the word *mass* can be applied at all to the tiny minority who read English; he is, after all, as widely read in India as, say, Agatha Christie.

Childhood is also, of course, a time for comics, and here American ones were greatly preferred to British. To an Indian child, the world portrayed in *Archie* or *Richie Rich* seemed infinitely more desirable than that of *Beano*. (Comics also made us aware of changing U.S. sensibilities. I still remember the first time black faces appeared on the Main Streets of comic strips, and what that taught me about the state of race relations in America.) The Classics Illustrated series was a sort of children's Reader's Digest Condensed Books, offering colorful capsule versions of more demanding literature, from *Huckleberry Finn* to *Around the World in Eighty Days*. But my favorite comics were the Belgian *Tintin* stories, brilliantly translated by the British team of Anthea Bell and Derek Hockridge. Hergé's perfectly sketched adventures of the boy reporter, his dog Snowy, and his sailor friend Captain Haddock (whose salty tongue produced delightfully polysyllabic invective — "bashi-bazouk!" "troglodyte!" "cercopithecus!") are classics of their kind. As clever, if not quite as thrilling, was the *Asterix* series, featuring an indomitable Gaulish village resisting Julius Caesar's Romans (who all bore appropriately Latinate names, from Marcus Ginantonicus to Crismus Bonus).

So mine was, all in all, an eclectic literary childhood. It is, I suppose, a uniquely Indian experience to embrace both Biggles and Birbal, Jeeves and the Jatakas, Tintin and

Tenaliraman, in your reading. Growing up as a reader in India left me with a vivid sense of books devoured as sources of entertainment, learning, escape — and vicarious experience.

The most difficult moments of my childhood came on one day every year, the holy day of Saraswati Puja. Hindus dedicated the day to the goddess of learning through prayer and ritual and, paradoxically, by denying themselves the joys of reading or writing. Despite the most strenuous efforts, I could never master the required degree of self-denial. If I successfully pushed my books aside, I would find myself reading the fine print on the toiletries in the bathroom or the fragments of old newspaper that lined my clothes drawers. But I think the goddess forgave me these transgressions. For I continued to read and to learn from books; and now she has even allowed me to write a few of them.

## 2

# Revenging Rudyard, Subverting Scarlett

E very writer nurtures an idle fantasy (some more than one!), a project they toss around from time to time in their minds but never actually get around to putting down on paper. In my case I have long wanted to exact a sort of postcolonial revenge on that archimperial literary figure, Rudyard Kipling, by subverting his overpraised novel *Kim*. Kipling's tale of the nineteenth-century British boy who grows up for some years as an Indian, wanders the streets picking up the languages, the habits, and the insights of the land, is restored to Englishness, and then returns years later as a British officer uniquely equipped to play the "Great Game" on behalf of the Raj seemed to me ripe for reversal. How about a novel, I mused, about an Indian boy — let us call him Mik — who, as a result of an albino birth or advanced leucoderma, is pale enough to pass off as a member of the melanin-deficient race that ruled us for two centuries? Mik might grow up in a British cantonment, be trained to rule at some British institution like Haileybury or Camberley, imbibe the ideas and attitudes (and understand the weaknesses) of the colonials, and then come back to India, rediscover his family and his roots, and turn his intimate knowledge of the oppressors against them as a fiery nationalist. I played with the notion for a while, but never got around to writing it.

But Mik came back to mind the other day when a literary controversy erupted in America over the proposed publication of a novel called *The Wind Done Gone*, which would seek to do to *Gone with the Wind* what I had wanted to do to *Kim*. The estate of Margaret Mitchell, whose only novel, *Gone with the Wind*, remains one of the most successful books (and movies) of all time, sued to prevent the publication of *The Wind Done Gone*, in which the same events are narrated from the point of view of a slave, the illegitimate half sister of Scarlett O'Hara. The author of *The Wind Done Gone*, Alice Randall, consciously sought to counter Mitchell's romanticized white-plantation South with an account from the perspective of the enslaved blacks who made the planters' prosperity possible. The Mitchell estate succeeded only briefly in getting a federal court to block publication of *The Wind Done Gone*, but the issue the case raises is an intriguing one. To the extent that literature captures our imagination with a version of experience that privileges a particular point of view, isn't it desirable, even essential, that others give voice to those who were voiceless, silent, marginal, even absent, in the original narrative?

Tom Stoppard, the brilliantly inventive British playwright, did precisely this in his early play *Rosencrantz and*

*Guildenstern Are Dead,* in which he took two minor characters from *Hamlet* and, in effect, rewrote Shakespeare by imagining the scenes the Bard left out, from the confused viewpoint of two hangers-on at Elsinore. Others, more recently, have done similar things. John Updike also reinvented *Hamlet* in his recent novel *Gertrude and Claudius.* In *Mary Reilly,* Valerie Martin retold Robert Louis Stevenson's *Dr. Jekyll and Mr. Hyde* from the point of view of the transformational doctor's maid. Herman Melville's classic *Moby-Dick,* with the obsessive Captain Ahab relentlessly pursuing the great white whale, underwent a feminist retelling in Sena Jeter Naslund's *Ahab's Wife.*

Shakespeare, Melville, and Stevenson are not merely safely dead, but gone so long that copyright on their stories has expired, which, alas for poor Ms. Randall, is not yet the case with *Gone with the Wind.* Indeed, a hugely controversial Italian novel by Pia Pera called *Lo's Diary* — which reimagines the tale of Vladimir Nabokov's *Lolita* from the point of view of the fourteen-year-old nymphet rather than that of the older man, Humbert, who was Nabokov's principal protagonist — is impossible to find in English. An attempted American edition was successfully killed off by the Nabokov estate, which went to court before the book was released commercially and had every copy pulped before it could be sold. The literary executors of authors usually claim to be acting to preserve the artistic integrity of the original work, which is certainly fair from a writer's point of view. But in the Mitchell case the argument is more legal than literary. It seems the Mitchell estate wants to assert its exclusive right to market spin-offs of the well-known characters, and might not be averse to licensing its own version of *Gone with the Wind* retold from a slave's point of view. It just doesn't want someone else cashing in on the idea.

The lethargy of our own courts aside, India strikes one at first glance as fertile soil for such reimaginings. When I took the liberty of reinventing the Mahabharata as a twentieth-century political satire in *The Great Indian Novel,* I rapidly learned of the many impeccable works in Indian languages that have already recast the epic, notably those that tell the tale from Draupadi's point of view rather than through the male gaze of the Pandavas. The Ramayana from Sita's perspective might tremble on the brink of sacrilege to some, and certainly one from Ravana's would bring the Bajrang Dal onto the streets, but how about more recent classics? That is where one stops short. So much of great Indian literature was already written to subvert the established order, to challenge the ruling narrative, that such an exercise seems otiose. The Kipling view of India was already countered in the 1930s by Mulk Raj Anand's *Coolie* and *Untouchable* and by Raja Rao's immortal *Kanthapura,* not to mention a host of works in Indian languages by Rabindranath Tagore, Munshi Premchand, Bankim Chandra Chatterjee, Subramania Bharati, and others too numerous to list, who used their writings explicitly to give a voice to those who had been marginalized by the imperial narrative. India's is already a literature of subversion, with the added distinction that the stories our great writers have told were entirely their own — they did not need to borrow from the canon to subvert it. We do not need to retell John Masters from the point of view of Mangal Pandey. We have already done better than John Masters ever could.

So I shall put Mik to rest for good. There are more interesting stories to be told, and they are always ours to tell.

# 3

# Mining the Mahabharata:
# Whose Culture Is It Anyway?

CONSIDER THE EVIDENCE. A television series retelling the Mahabharata is the most successful Indian TV program ever, drawing an audience of over 200 million and paralyzing life during the hours of its weekly telecast. The Western world's leading avant-garde theater director makes a nine-hour play of the epic, which a multinational cast performs to enthusiastic acclaim across the globe, from Avignon to Ayers Rock. Shorter TV and film versions of the play are also successfully distributed worldwide. The best-selling book in the history of Indian publishing in English is not some steamy potboiler, but the venerable C. Rajagopalachari ("Rajaji")'s episodic translation of the Mahabharata. (If the sales of other translations were added, the Mahabharata would probably eclipse the next few Indian best-sellers put together.) Obviously, the two-thousand-year-old epic is still flourishing: why, an American professor in Washington, D.C., offers a "multimedia" course in the Mahabharata, with students examining it from a dozen different contemporary perspectives, including those of Bollywood, Peter Brook — and yours truly.

Which immodest reference brings me to the book at hand, my first novel, immodestly (but not entirely immodestly, as I shall explain) titled *The Great Indian Novel*. It is precisely the epic's appeal to non-Sanskrit scholars that has ensured the Mahabharata's present-day relevance and given me material for my novel. I am no expert on the great epic, but *The Great Indian Novel* draws extensively from it. (Including its name: as I explain in an author's note at the very beginning of the book, its title is not a reflection of my estimate of its contents, but a reference to this source of inspiration — for since *maha* means "great" and *Bharat* is the Hindi name for India, *Mahabharata*, after all, can be read to mean "Great India.") I have, to put it simply, used the Mahabharata as a vehicle for an attempt to retell the political history of twentieth-century India, through a fictional recasting of its events, episodes, and characters.

*The Great Indian Novel* is preceded by three epigraphs that frame and underpin this endeavor: the first from the eminent Mahabharata scholar C. R. Deshpande, attesting to the importance of the epic in the Indian consciousness ("it has moulded the very character of the Indian people"); the second from its most creative translator, P. Lal, reiterating the case for its contemporary relevance (and quoted more fully below); and the third from a non-Indian writer, Günter Grass, urging that "writers experience another view of history" and that "literature must refresh memory." My novel stands at the intersection of these three ideas.

There is a considerable basis for Deshpande's view

amongst Sanskrit scholars in the classical canon. The grand old man of Mahabharata studies, V. S. Sukthankar, put it uncompromisingly: "The Mahabharata," he wrote, "is the content of our collective unconscious. . . . We must therefore grasp this great book with both hands and face it squarely. Then we shall recognize that it is our past which has prolonged itself into the present. We are it." Another eminent scholar, R. N. Dandekar, pointed out that "men and women in India from one end of the country to the other, whether young or old, whether rich or poor, whether high or low, whether simple or sophisticated, still derive entertainment, inspiration, and guidance from the Mahabharata. . . . There is indeed no department of Indian life, public or private, which is not effectively influenced by the great epic. It would not be an exaggeration to say that the people of India have learnt to think and act in terms of the Mahabharata."

Lal takes this a crucial step further:

> The epic of Vyasa is not a literary masterpiece out there, somewhere in the past, or tucked away in air-conditioned museums and libraries. Its characters still walk the Indian streets, its animals populate our forests, its legends and myths haunt and inspire the Indian imagination, its events are the disturbing warp and woof of our age. . . . The essential Mahabharata is whatever is relevant to us in the second half of the twentieth century; whatever helps us understand and live better our own Dharma, *Artha*, Kama and *Moksha* [faith, wealth, pleasure and salvation]. . . . No epic, no work of art, is sacred by itself; if it does not have meaning for me now, it is nothing, it is dead.

Lal's view underscores, rather than undermines, the traditionalists' position. The Mahabharata has come to stand for so much in the popular consciousness of Indians: the issues the epic raises, as well as the values it seeks to promote, are central to an understanding of what makes India India. And yet the Mahabharata is a tale of the real world, one whose heroes have feet of clay, whose stories have ambiguous ends, whose events range from great feats of honor and valor to dubious compromises, broken promises, dishonorable battles, expedient lies, dispensable morality. That made it ideal for my own purposes as a novelist. To take characters and situations that are laden with epic resonance, and to alter and shape them to tell a contemporary story, was a challenge that offered a rare opportunity to strike familiar chords while playing an unfamiliar tune.

In my view the Mahabharata is an ideal vehicle for my own modest efforts to affirm and enhance an Indian cultural identity, not as a closed or self-limiting construct, but as a reflection of the pluralism, diversity, and openness of India's kaleidoscopic culture. In the process it aims to broaden understanding of the Indian cultural and historical heritage while reclaiming for Indians the story of India's experience with foreign rule and its nationalist reassertion, including the triumphs and disappointments of freedom.

In making this case, I am conscious of the need for a key caveat. This relates to my use of the terms *India* and *Indians*. In his magisterial essay on life and culture in Mexico, *The Labyrinth of Solitude*, Octavio Paz observed that his thoughts were not concerned with the entire Mexican population but rather with those among them "who are conscious of themselves, for one reason or another, as Mexicans." The same applies, for comparable reasons, today, for I speak of an India that exists in the awareness of most, but not all, of my countrymen and -women. Paz went on to serve as Mexico's ambassador to India in the 1960s, and I imagine he saw that, as in the Mexico he was writing about in 1950, several historical epochs and states of development coexist simultaneously in India. This is still the case, and it would be foolish as well as presumptuous to seek to speak for them all in a general notion of Indianness. In the last fifty years not all Indians have learned to think of themselves as Indians, and to speak of an Indian cultural identity is really to subsume a number of identities, varying depending upon class, caste, region, and language. But this variety is in itself integral to my idea of Indianness: the singular thing about India is that you can only speak of it in the plural. Given the extraordinary mixture of ethnic groups, the profusion of mutually incomprehensible languages, the varieties of topography and climate, the diversity of religions and cultural practices, and the range of levels of economic development that India embraces, India is fundamentally a pluralist state: its pluralism emerges from its geography, is reflected in its history, and is confirmed by its ethnography. Indian culture is therefore by definition a culture of multiplicities, a culture of differences.

A British friend, asked to explain to a foreigner what made England England, replied, "cricket, Shakespeare, the BBC." Though so concise an answer would be difficult for an Indian, it is impossible to imagine any similar attempt to describe India that omits the Mahabharata. The Mahabharata declares, "What is here is nowhere else; what is not here, is nowhere." Few other works in world literature could make such an extravagant claim, but in doing so, the two-thousand-year-old Indian epic poem is not defending a closed structure: rather, the Mahabharata has had so many accretions over the years in constant retellings that there is practically no subject it does not cover. Its characters and personages still march triumphantly in Indian minds, its myths and legends still inspire the Indian imagination, its events still speak to Indians with a contemporary resonance rare in many twentieth-century works. The basic story, if the tale of the dynastic rivalry between the Pandava and Kaurava clans may be called that, has been so thoroughly the object of adaptation, interpolation, and reinterpretation that the Mahabharata as we now have it overflows with myths and legends of all sorts, didactic tales exalting the Brahmins, fables and stories that teach moral and existential lessons, bardic poetry extolling historical dynasties, and meandering digressions on everything from law to lechery and politics to philosophy. Whenever a particular social or political message was sought to be imparted to Indians at large, it was simply inserted into a retelling of the Mahabharata. As Rajaji (C. Rajagopalachari) dryly put it, "Interpolation in a recognized classic seemed to correspond to inclusion in the national library." This elasticity through the ages adds to the timelessness of the epic's appeal.

But Lal's proposition raises a larger question: what exactly in the Mahabharata is "relevant to us in the second half of the twentieth century"?

Lal himself has an intriguing answer. Vyasa, he says, "posits an intricate dharma, where right and wrong are bewilderingly mixed. . . . [His] epic is a mirror in which the Indian sees himself undeceived." The Mahabharata is a tale of the real world, one whose heroes have feet of clay. "The anguished intensity of the Indian's involvement with the Mahabharata can be seen in the way reference is made to the epic in public life. The Ramayana is cited generally when ethical ideals are expected; the Mahabharata is referred to when compromises are made, shady deals struck, promises dishonored, battles fought, disasters lamented." And indeed, which Indian, perusing the incessant political reports that dominate our national newspapers, has not come across references to great conflicts as Kurukshetras, heroes as Arjuns, villains as Kauravas? The Mahabharata is an unending source of metaphor for the rhetoric of our public debate. Indian politicians are ever ready to portray themselves as Yudhishtira, to warn overbold rivals that they are Abhimanyus trapped in *padmavyuhams* (lotus rings) of their own making, or to depict misguided senior statesmen as Bhishmas (men who provide, as Mrs. Gandhi said of Morarji Desai's stand on the abolition of privy purses, "a moral facade to an indefensible case.")

But Lal's argument is not merely at the metaphorical level, though he dwells with great relish on these and similar examples. The Mahabharata, he says, "is our Doomsday Epic," depicting a period of "moral collapse" comparable to that of our times: "The Mahabharata is recommended reading for an age that breeds dry thoughts in a Waste Land, speculates fascinatedly on the paradoxical Black Holes of interstellar space, and cannot be sure if there will indeed be a 2001 for mankind beyond the Holocaust."

Lal finds interesting support for this view in the French dramatist who wrote Peter Brook's "international" version of the epic, Jean-Claude Carrière. "This immense poem," Carrière wrote in 1985, "which flows with the majesty of a great river, carries an inexhaustible richness which defies all structural, thematic, historical or psychological analysis. . . . Layers of ramifications, sometimes contradictory, follow up on one another and are interwoven without losing the central theme. That theme is a threat: we live in a time of destruction — everything points in the same direction."

Carrière may well have been thinking of the Cold War still raging at the time, but his point is fair enough even today: in an India of erupting caste and communal conflict, terrorist and secessionist strife, police "encounters" and an alarming daily toll of human lives in the aftermath of the destruction of the Babri Masjid or the near-pogroms in Gujarat, any work that speaks of a "time of destruction" cannot but be considered relevant. No wonder that so many contemporary poets, dramatists, and novelists, writing in every Indian language, have found inspiration in episodes of the Mahabharata, which they have retold in a variety of ways. But the message is not a purely negative one. In the face of destruction, the Mahabharata offers a valid response, in the Bhagavad Gita's affirmation of disinterested action. Lal, indeed, argues that "the *Mahabharata* is an epic of action" and that its "core moral . . . is to show the primacy of action."

The events of the epic, as they unfold, offer other straws for drowning modern optimists to clutch. Rajaji saw the epic as pointing to "the vanity of ambition and the evil and futility of anger and hatred." C. V. Narasimhan, then a senior United Nations official, went further, identifying a "theme of peace and reconciliation" in the Mahabharata that had "a special application" in the days of the Cold War (and perhaps even more so in an era in which a hot peace, littered with little wars, has broken out at the end of the Cold War). Professor Barbara Stoler Miller, Peter Brook's scholarly consultant on the play, declared that "the purpose of the Mahabharata is to teach that good ultimately triumphs, even in a time of cosmic destructiveness." Lal himself, after focusing on the didacticism of the Bhagavad Gita, added to his analysis the point that "the end of the Mahabharata underlines the futility of revengeful warfare and restores the validity of Arjuna's compassion."

What do these contradictory exegeses suggest about the message of the Mahabharata in today's India? They reflect, certainly, the undeniable fact that the great epic, like many great epics, has the capacity to be all things to all men. The hubristic claim for the epic, in its own words — "What is here is nowhere else; what is not here, is nowhere" — was thus quite literally true, at least over the thousand years the epic took to arrive at its settled shape in around A.D. 500. Whereas the classical Indian *sastras* were treatises on *artha* (wealth), dharma (faith), *kama* (pleasure), or *moksha* (salvation), the Mahabharata, uniquely, is simultaneously *arthasastra, dharmasastra, kamasastra,* and *mokshasastra* — a "fifth Veda," as it has been called, of material and spiritual, physical and metaphysical, life, but unlike the other four a secular rather than religious work, a Veda of the Indian masses. Some scholars consider the eclecticism of the epic valuable:

Father Robert Antoine, that remarkable Jesuit Sanskritist, saw in the Mahabharata "a mirror of Indian life throughout several centuries, a mirror in which popular beliefs, social customs, religious practice and speculation, folklore, civil and criminal law are reflected." Others, like R. C. Dutt, were less charmed, seeing the congeries of elements as an unattractive jumble. Either way, to distill a single absolute message from the epic as a whole seems to me a disingenuous exercise. The Mahabharata offers enough textual evidence for practically any conclusion you wish to derive from it.

Look at some of the issues the epic has been cited on in recent years. The great climax of Kurukshetra and its aftermath have given the Mahabharata its standing as the great tale of war and destruction, an urgent reminder of the perils of the nuclear age. The discussion between Krishna and Arjun in the Bhagavad Gita has been seen variously as upholding righteous war, rejecting pacifism, underlining compassion, articulating an ethic of action, and stressing the importance of duty, including caste duty. Draupadi's challenge to the male elders when she is "lost" by Yudhishtira in the game of dice has been hailed as a spirited battle cry for women's rights; but others have recalled that the epic, at least in its southern recension, demeans and belittles women (in C. R. Deshpande's words, the Mahabharata claims that "if a man has one thousand tongues, lives for a hundred years, and does nothing except describe the faults of woman, he will die without finishing the job"). Many of the values and mores of the epic would be seen as illegal, immoral, or impractical today. Controversy still rages in the popular press over whether Draupadi "really" had five husbands;

the text can be read to mean that she was married to all of them, but also to support the conservative view that she was only married to the eldest, Yudhishtira (the only one whose freedom she asked for when Dhritarashtra offered her a boon). Before any inferences are drawn from that for contemporary society, there is the fact that polyandry is still practiced in the Jaunsar Babar region of Uttar Pradesh. On the grander questions, the Mahabharata offers a variety of thoughts on the meaning of life and death: episodes like Bhishma's death and Yudhishtira's vision of hell offer rich material, not all of it internally consistent.

Which brings me to my point: the Mahabharata is what you make of it. Its relevance to today's India is the relevance that today's Indians want to see in it. After all, the epic has, throughout the ages, been the object of adaptation, interpolation, reinterpretation, and expurgation by a number of retellers, each seeking to reflect what he saw as relevant to his time. Its contemporary retellings — whether B. R. Chopra's soap-operatic version on television or mine in satirical fiction — merely confirm the Mahabharata's traditional status as the repository of the national myth. This includes the stories, the ideas, the social and political customs and practices, the prescriptions and values, that the reteller considers significant to his retelling.

In this sense, to retell the Mahabharata is simply to recall the kind of stories Indian society tells about itself. In many cultures, myths and epics both contribute to and reflect the national consciousness. India's has inevitably changed in the two thousand years since the original Mahabharata was composed. What, I asked myself, would a twentieth-century Ved Vyas tell about his India, about the great events of his times? So I used the great epic as the framework for a satirical reworking of the major Indian political events of this century, from the days of British colonial rule to the struggle for freedom and the triumphs and disappointments of independence. In the process, I tried to reject some old assumptions, derived as much from the colonial view of India as from India's own uncritically accepted versions of our past. In my story I have set out to explore what has made India and nearly unmade it, and to consider the nature of truth in life as in fiction, in tradition as in history.

The choice of historical events to portray was easily made. The mode of their portrayal was another matter. That the Mahabharata characters and episodes mean something to most Indians added a dimension to the fiction that the novelist's craft alone could not convey. In applying the story of Gandhari (the epic heroine who tied a blindfold over her eyes in order not to see more of the world than her blind husband) to the much-sacrificing, neglected wife of a visionary nationalist, or in changing the outcome of the fight with the demon Bakasura to mirror the nature of the Sino-Indian War, I am borrowing from ancient tradition to make a point about recent history.

At the same time I did not want to descend to the national tendency of hagiology: dealing with subjects as sensitive as tradition and history, I judged a degree of irreverence to be essential in the telling. All the more so, indeed, since I would be exploring potentially portentous themes. I took heart from the conviction that irreverence in the Indian tradition is not sacrilege: as the Mahabharata amply demonstrates, the epics themselves ascribe human qualities, imperfections, base motives, and feet of clay even to the gods.

Of course my irreverence is not an end in itself. In the area of style, for instance, I frequently broke into light verse, and not merely for amusement; I was deliberately recalling the fact that many translators of the Mahabharata, defeated in their attempts to convey the special quality of the world's longest epic poem, have tried to combine prose and poetry in their renditions, with varying degrees of success. My various literary and less-than-literary devices serve an attempt to look at Indian political history through the refraction of two different kinds of light. One is, of course, the light cast by the past, by the values taught to us in our mythology, by the examples set by the Mahabharata. The other is the light cast by a satirical view of the present, which by deliberate simplification and fictionalization (one might even say conscious distortion) throws certain trends and issues into sharper relief than history makes possible. This certainly applies to the real-life "parallels" with the Mahabharata that reviewers have been quick to seize upon, but it is also valid where no parallel exists. To me, for instance, the upright Yudhishtir's smugness and hypocrisy found a contemporary echo in a recent political figure, while the Ekalavya story (where the lower-caste boy, who has mastered archery by eavesdropping on Drona's classes, cuts off his thumb on Drona's demand) had to be changed to make a twentieth-century point.

At the same time the yoking of the Mahabharata to modern history restricted some of my fictional options: as the novel progressed, I was obliged to abandon novelistic conventions and develop some characters who are walking metaphors. Draupadi, thus, became emblematic of Indian democracy, her attempted disrobing a symbol of what was sought to be done to democracy not so long ago. Equally, the story of Jarasandha, the king who was defeated by being torn in two and flung in different directions, mirrored the 1971 breaking up of Pakistan.

All this needed a style as varied in tone, form, and scansion as the epic itself, with its numerous interpolations and digressions: the story of India, like that of the Mahabharata, had to come across as a tale of many tellers, even if it is ascribed only to one.

This is why I agree with the critic who has suggested that *The Great Indian Novel* "speaks for an India of multiple realities, and of multiple interpretations of reality." So, I would suggest, does the epic; and so does Indian culture, that elusive construct. Throughout my novel runs an acknowledgment of the multiplicity of truth, and a conscious evocation of the many truths that have helped give shape and substance to the idea of India. My fiction is infused, in this sense, with the "greatness" of India, of Maha Bharata, a greatness that has emerged from the fusion of its myths with the aspirations of its history.

My motivation is a conscious one. Most developing countries are also formerly colonized countries, and one of the realities of colonialism is that it appropriated the cultural definition of its subject peoples. Writing about India in English, I cannot but be aware of those who have done the same before me, others with a greater claim to the language but a lesser claim to the land. Think of India in the English-speaking world even today, and you think in images conditioned by Rudyard Kipling and E. M. Forster, by the Bengal Lancers and *The Jewel in the Crown*. But their stories are not my stories, their heroes are not mine; and my fiction seeks to reclaim my country's heritage for itself, to tell, in an Indian voice, a story of India. Let me stress, a story of India; for there are always other stories, and other Indians to tell them.

Of course, mine is an Indian voice in the English language: our multiple identity is expressed in a multiplicity of tongues. At the same time, as an English-language writer, I acknowledge that the colonial connection also helped us find our Indian voice. Early in the novel, a British official remarks, "Basic truth about the colonies, Heaslop. Any time there's trouble, you can put it down to books. Too many of the wrong ideas getting into the heads of the wrong sorts of people. If ever the Empire comes to ruin, Heaslop, mark my words, the British publisher will be to blame." (It was no accident that my novel was first published by a British publisher!)

And so my allusions are not only to Indian myths, ancient and modern. I have tried, in the story, in its metaphors and in stray references throughout the text, to take account of other fictional attempts to depict the Indo-British encounter. (Which is why there are chapters called "Passages through India" and "The Bungle Book" — and even, in another sly dig at Kipling, "Him.") It is no accident that the fictional re-creation of the Jallianwala Bagh massacre in this novel takes place at the Bibigarh Gardens. Paul Scott took the Bibigarh (the site of the massacre of English civilians in 1857) from Indian history to make it the site of the rape of Daphne Manners by several Indians in his otherwise admirable *The Jewel in the Crown*. I am hardly the first to point out that the use by both Scott and E. M. Forster of rape as a metaphor for the colonial connection is a bit odd, since the facts of imperialism would suggest that if any violation occurred, it was of India by the English, and not the other way around. So I reclaimed the Bibigarh Gardens for my side, as it were, by casting it as the location for a historical massacre of Indian civilians by British troops.

No name in the book, not even of a minor character or place, is casually chosen: each is derived either from the epic itself (Lord Drewpad, for instance, is an anglicization of King Drupad) or from writings (and writers — Kipling, Scott, A. L. Basham, Beverly Nichols) about India, unless it is a direct reference to real geography (Comea is obviously Goa, Hangari Das a personification of Hungary during the 1956 Soviet invasion, and so on).

So in reminding readers of an epic past, I am not writing of some atavistic view of India, an India of distant greatness untouched by the rest of the world. In fact the sensibility from which my narrator speaks is an eclectic one, heir to centuries of Hindu, Muslim, and colonial rule. At the same time, I see his telling of this story as a part of the challenge of post-Independence development, a narrative to set alongside the railway lines, the steel mills, the space stations, of the new India.

The novel begins with the proposition that India is not, as people keep calling it, an underdeveloped country but rather, in the context of its history and cultural heritage, a highly developed one in an advanced state of decay. Such sentiments are, of course, the privilege of the satirist; but the notion of decay apart, I am trying to remind readers of

an India that was indeed highly developed once — an India
that evolved a settled civilization five thousand years ago,
an India whose level of art, architecture, literature, and philosophy made it perhaps the most developed country on
earth in 300 B.C., an India that invented the zero and the
decimal system, an India that evolved two major systems of
classical music and five of classical dance, developed highly
sophisticated techniques of medicine and meditation, exported silk and spices, and was the birthplace of four of the
world's major religious faiths as well as home to many more.
I could go on, but I am not seeking to romanticize a mythic
past; rather, when my cantankerous old narrator declares, at
the beginning of the novel, that "everything in India is
overdeveloped," he is deliberately provoking his readers to
forget their usual view of an underdeveloped country as one
devoid of everything the material world today generally values. In the telling of the story of India, I try to evoke an idea
of development that transcends — but does not deny —
the conventional socioeconomic indices.

I realize I may be providing fodder for those who have
penned learned analyses about some Indian writers' "anxiety
of Indianness." To me, my Indianness is not a matter of anxiety. I see cultural reassertion (the reassertion of a pluralist
Indian culture) as a vital part of the enormous challenges
confronting a country like India — as vital as economic development. We are all familiar with the notion that "man does
not live by bread alone." In India, I would argue that music,
dance, art, and the telling of stories are indispensable to our
ability to cope with the human condition. After all, why
does man need bread? To survive. But why survive, if it is

only to eat more bread? To live is more than just to sustain life — it is to enrich, and be enriched by, life. Our poorest men and women feel the throb of culture on their pulse, for they tell stories to their children under the starlit skies — stories of their land and its heroes, stories of the earth and its mysteries, stories that have gone into making them what they are. And (as I suggested in my second novel, *Show Business*) they see and hear stories too, in the flickering lights of the thousands of cinemas in our land, where myth and escapist fantasy intertwine and moral righteousness almost invariably triumphs with the closing credits. In India and elsewhere, there is no "development" without fiction.

Without culture, development becomes mere materialism, a set of figures on GNP tables, a subject for economists and planners rather than a matter of people. And if people are to develop, it is unthinkable that they would develop without culture, without song, and dance, and music, and myth, without stories about themselves, and in turn, without expressing their views on their present lot and their future hopes. Development implies dynamism; dynamism requires freedom, the freedom to create; creativity is both a condition and a guarantee of culture. This is why it is worth retelling our ancient stories in new and original ways — why literature, as Grass would have it, must refresh memory. As we hurtle into the twenty-first century, we need ways of remembering all that happened in the previous twenty (or in India's case, the previous thirty-five).

As a novelist, I believe in distracting in order to instruct — my novels are, to some degree, didactic works masquerading as entertainments. I subscribe to Molière's credo, "Le devoir de la comédie est de corriger les hommes en les divertissant." You have to entertain in order to edify. But edify to what end? What is the responsibility of the creative artist, the writer, in a developing society? In this exegesis about my own novel I have pointed to one responsibility — to contribute toward, and to help articulate and give expression to, the cultural identity (shifting, variegated, and multiple, in the Indian case) of our postcolonial society. The vast majority of developing countries have emerged recently from the incubus of colonialism, which has in many ways fractured and distorted their cultural self-perceptions. Development will not occur without a reassertion of identity: that this is who we are, this is what has made us, this is what we are proud of, this is what we want to be. In this process, culture and development are fundamentally linked and interdependent. The task of the creative artist is to find new ways (and revive old ones) of expressing his or her culture, just as society strives, through development, to find new ways of being and becoming.

In reiterating the epic, the reteller and his audience are recalling the shaping of their own cultural identity. Yet it is this identity-asserting quality of the Mahabharata that has also, to some observers, made it dangerous in contemporary India. "For the lost generation of today," wrote the cultural commentator Chidananda DasGupta, "a generation that has become incapable of reading it in [the] original and too impatient even to read complete translations, the degraded version on television . . . is still a revelation of an unsuspected facet of our national heritage." In the process, DasGupta regretted that the votaries of Hindutva had laid claim to it,

34

"that one of the world's greatest and most universal epics should be reduced to the religious text of a community." The writer Sukumar Mitra, deploring the "transfigurement" of the epic "into a religio-didactic spectacle," saw a sinister purpose behind the TV-inspired Mahabharata revival:

> The message is that modern Bharata must be turned again into a "dharmakshetra-kurukshetra" . . . to regain for the saints and God's chosen communities the right to perform selfless karma. . . . In the present troubled state of Bharat, God's agents, aided by an enthusiastic Doordarshan, are stirring up 82% of the country's souls to the doom of the rest, to receive their redeemer . . . for the re-establishment of dharma.

The reestablishment of dharma, properly understood, in and of itself is hardly disturbing as a prospect (and I have urged it in my 1997 book *India: From Midnight to the Millennium*), but that was not what Mitra meant; his concern was that the televised epic would become a vehicle for Hindu chauvinism. That would indeed have been worrying, if true (a qualification made necessary by the fact that the TV *Mahabharata* was written by a Muslim dialogist, Rahi Masoom Reza, and its production values may have had more to do with Bollywood kitsch than with Hindu atavism.) In any case, there is little doubt about a national trend toward the increasing communalization of religious faith, a trend that the ancient epics are inevitably being called upon to serve. In the case of the Mahabharata, this is particularly ironic. During a literary reading in New Delhi in 1991, I was asked whether I was not worried about helping to revive the epic at a time when fanatics of various stripes were reasserting "Hindu pride" in aggressive and exclusionist terms. I responded that to me, the Mahabharata, unlike the explicitly religious Ramayana, is a purely secular epic; its characters (with the sole exception of Krishna) are not divine, and their deeds are as human, and as capable of greatness and debasement, as those of any of our contemporary heroes. And, as befits a truly Indian epic, there is nothing restrictive or self-limiting about the Indian identity it reasserts: it is large, eclectic, and flexible, containing multitudes.

I am glad that *The Great Indian Novel* is still being reprinted and read nearly sixteen years after I wrote it, and that my Indian publishers have seen fit to publish a special commemorative edition of it on the occasion of the fiftieth anniversary of India's independence from British rule. If there is a message to the book, a message I have derived from the Mahabharata, it is twofold. First, that of the need to reexamine all received wisdom about India, to question the certitudes, to acknowledge the imperfections and face them; second, to do so through a reassertion of dharma, defined not just as religion but as the whole complex of values and standards — some derived from myth and tradition, some derived from our history — by which India and Indians must live. In this approach — which is, of course, no more and no less valid than any of those through which other conclusions have been drawn for today's India — I hope I have been faithful to the spirit of the Mahabharata, despite all the other liberties I have taken with it. And I hope, of course, to have demonstrated its continued relevance once again.

# 4

# In Defense of the Bollywood Novel

A CLASSIC *NEW YORKER* CARTOON shows a writer floundering in choppy water, stretching hopelessly out toward an inner tube floating just beyond the reach of his flailing hand. A typewriter sits in it, on whose solitary page can be seen the words "Second Novel." Few challenges are quite as prone to generating literary anxiety as that of producing a second novel, especially when the first has been reasonably well-received.

After *The Great Indian Novel*, a lot of readers didn't know what next to expect from me, but many in India made it clear that a novel about the Hindi film world called *Show Business* wasn't quite it. The book was reviewed on the front page of the *New York Times Book Review* and enjoyed raves elsewhere, but in India the disappointment was palpable — the author of *The Great Indian Novel* writing about something as trivial as Bollywood? I was soon being asked whether I had abandoned the larger themes and serious issues that I had taken up with my first novel.

It was odd having to explain that *Show Business* also deals with some fairly serious questions — reality and illusion, morality and human values, life and death, the life of the surface versus the interior life. In my view, any subject, pretty much, can lend itself to serious fictional inquiry, and that includes the life and times of a Bollywood film star. *The Great Indian Novel* took on a two-thousand-year-old epic and all of twentieth century Indian history, but it was hardly reasonable to expect each of my novels to be painted on the same vast canvas. One is always looking for new creative metaphors to explore the Indian condition, and cinema was a particularly useful one. In addition, some interesting issues emerged from the subject itself: the social and political relevance of popular cinema in India, for instance, had been dealt with surprisingly little in Indo-Anglian fiction. And the whole process of the manufacture of our modern myths on celluloid was one that I found fascinating as a creative issue in itself: How were these stories told? What do they mean to those who make them and those who see them? How do they relate to their lives?

One critic wondered why, one book after being hailed as India's first post-modern writer, I had written what some might consider to be a more conventional novel. I don't care about the "post-modern" stuff myself — these labels are for the critics to devise, and I certainly did not see myself through them. But in fact *Show Business* was not all that conventional. I have always believed that, as the very word "novel" suggests, there must be something new or innovative about every novel one sets out to write: otherwise, what would be the point? In the case of *Show Business* it had to do mainly with the way the novel unfolds. There are three interlocking narratives in each of the sections of the book, or "takes," as I called them. The first is the first-person narrative of my protagonist, the Bollywood film star himself, recalling episodes from six different points of his life. The novel begins with him shooting his first film, and ends with him on his deathbed. The second narrative is the story, complete with tongue-in-cheek lyrics, of the formula movie he's acting in at the time, along with other characters from the novel. The third narrative is a series of second-person monologues, addressed to him in the hospital by each of these characters: the "villain," the hero's father and brother, his mistress, his wife. The story of the novel emerges through the interweaving of these three narratives. I do like my readers to work a little for their pleasure!

As a writer, I have always believed that the way I tell the story is as important as the story itself. The manner in which the narrative unfolds is as integral to the novel as the story it tells, and as essential, I hope, to the experience of the reader. That said, I don't think novelists should spend too much time rationalizing their whimsies. I basically write as it comes to me. In this novel, the style and structure served to juxtapose different perceptions, which was important to the substance of the story.

Nor did the novel abandon the political concerns of my literary debut. There is some political satire in *Show Business* — even the title is deliberately ambiguous, and refers to politics and religion, as well as to the hero's personal life, not just his film career. The connection between politics and film in India is one of the themes the novel explores — within, of course, its fictional parameters. My basic approach in the novel was still that of the satirist: though my novel revolves around one principal character, my concern is not for the man but the mores, and less for the individual than the issues.

But there was another aspect to what I had done differently — a question, I suppose, of scale affecting substance. In *The Great Indian Novel*, in the process of yoking history to myth, I had to resort, especially in the last third of the book, to characters who were largely walking metaphors. In the new novel I tried instead to portray human beings of much greater complexity — with their fears, lusts, deceits, needs, frustrations. I was writing a book in which nothing is really what it seems. The hero isn't really a hero, because he's vain, selfish, incompetent, insensitive and unfaithful, but he gets some of the most beguiling, even likeable, narrative in the book.

The initials of the hero's name — Ashok Banjara, A. B. — inevitably attracted comment, as suggesting a real-life parallel to the legendary Bombay film star Amitabh Bachhan. There were certainly characters and situations in the novel that might strike a familiar chord in some Indian readers' minds. But the name "Ashok Banjara" was, in fact, a pseudonym I used during my freshman days in college, when the magazine *JS* thought I needed to be protected against the likely consequences of articles I wrote attacking "ragging" (hazing) on the Delhi University campus. And, at the risk of seeming disingenuous, Amitabh Bachhan is quite deliberately mentioned once or twice in the novel as a separate person, a rival of Ashok Banjara.

At the same time it is true that I have used real life, or some aspects of it, as a sort of a launching pad for my fiction. It's hardly an uncommon technique; Salman Rushdie, for instance, has often resorted to the same device. It's exhilarating, in some ways, to bounce yourself off real life while being free to soar above fact. The career of any of our film stars may not be the stuff of great literature, but elements from it may suggest themes it is appropriate, even vital, for literature to explore. After all, as my novel suggests, art imitates life, and in Bollywood, life returns the compliment.

# 5

# A Novel of Collisions

THERE IS NOTHING QUITE LIKE THE THRILL of publishing a
book, though mothers have probably come closest to
the experience in having a baby. (Much the same combination of emotions is involved — the thrill of conception, the
anxiety of nurturing the spark into full-blown life, the ex-
hausted satisfaction of delivery.) As I write these words I
have before me two different editions of my new novel
*Riot* — the Indian edition from Viking Penguin, with a
stark, powerful cover photograph of a scene from a real riot,
with flames and smoke arising from an overturned cart; and
the American edition from Arcade, black and red and gold,
with an elegiac photograph of the sun setting behind a
Mughal monument, bordered with colorful Rajasthani fret-
work. The Indian edition reflects the publishers' focus on
the political themes with which the book engages; the
American edition evokes an older, gentler image of India,
and is subtitled "A Love Story." My Indian friends all prefer the Indian cover; my American friends are much more

attracted to the American. So clearly both publishers know their markets well.

The two covers reflect, too, two different aspects of the same novel, because *Riot* is a love story, while also being a hate story. That is to say, it is the story of two people intimately in love in a little district town in Uttar Pradesh, but it also a story of the smoldering hatreds being stoked in that town, Zalilgarh, and of the conflagration in which both are (also intimately) caught up. American readers looking for a love story will also find a novel about the construction of identity, the nature of truth, and the ownership of history; Indian readers expecting a novel about the dangers of communalism will also discover a tale of another kind of passion.

Both are central to the novel's purpose. I am conscious that, in India, critics expect a serious writer to be "ambitious," something that some felt I had failed to be in my second novel, *Show Business*, which came in the wake of *The Great Indian Novel*. I believe *Riot* is ambitious in its own way — *The Great Indian Novel* took an epic sweep across the entire political history of twentieth-century India while reinventing the Mahabharata in the same breath, while *Riot* seeks to examine some of the most vital issues of our day on a smaller, more intimate canvas. Who is to say whether the work of the landscape artist is more ambitious than that of the miniaturist? As I said somewhat testily to an interviewer the other day, I'd like to think that all my books are, in their own ways, extremely ambitious — otherwise, with everything else I have to do already in my life and work, what would be the point in writing them?

The fact is that I had become increasingly concerned

with the communal issues bedeviling our national politics and society in the 1990s, and I wrote extensively about them in my newspaper columns and in my last book, *India: From Midnight to the Millennium.* This was all in the nature of commentary. As a novelist, though, I sought an interesting way to explore the issue in fiction. Years ago, my old college friend Harsh Mander, an IAS (Indian Administrative Service) officer, sent me an account he had written of a riot he dealt with as a district magistrate in Madhya Pradesh. I was very moved by the piece and urged him to publish it, and I am very pleased that a collection of Harsh's essays about the "forgotten people" he has dealt with in his career has just emerged from Penguin under the title *Unheard Voices.* But his story also sparked me thinking of a riot as a vehicle for a novel about communal hatred. Since I have never managed a riot myself, I asked Harsh for permission to use the story of "his" riot in my narrative, a request to which he graciously consented. At about the same time, I read a newspaper account of a young white American girl, Amy Biehl, who had been killed by a black mob in violent disturbances in South Africa. The two images stayed and merged in my mind, and *Riot* was born.

I began writing it in December 1996, immediately after completing *India: From Midnight to the Millennium.* But in view of the various demands on my time with my work at the United Nations, I could only complete it four years later, around the end of 2000. In between, whole months went by during which I was unable to touch the novel. With fiction, you need not only time — which I am always struggling to find — but also a space inside your head, to create an alternative universe and to inhabit it so intimately that its reality infuses your awareness of the world. That is all the more difficult when your daily obligations and responsibilities are so onerous that they are constantly pressing in on you, and you don't have a clear stretch of time to immerse yourself in your fictional universe.

*Riot* is also a departure for me fictionally, because unlike my earlier novels it is not a satirical work. Like the other two, though, it takes liberties with the fictional form. I have always believed that the very word *novel* implies that there must be something "new" about each one. What was new to me about the way *Riot* unfolded was that I told the story through newspaper clippings, diary entries, interviews, transcripts, journals, scrapbooks, even poems written by the characters — in other words, using different voices, different stylistic forms, for different fragments of the story. (It is also a book you can read in any order: though ideally you should read it from beginning to end, you can pick it up from any chapter, go back or forward to any other chapter, and bring a different level of awareness to the story.)

The story of *Riot* was a story of various kinds of collisions — of people, of cultures, ideologies, loves, hatreds — and it could not be told from just one point of view. The challenge I set myself in writing this book was not just to imagine a dozen different characters but to try and enter their imaginations; in other words, to see the world through their eyes. In describing Zalilgarh from the perspective of "Mrs. Hart," for instance, I had not just to visualize the town, a town like many I have seen throughout India, but to ask myself what a middle-aged, intelligent, but fairly conservative

American woman would notice about it. Similarly I sought to depict four or five different people's views of the Ram Janmabhoomi/Babri Masjid controversy; despite my own strong feelings about it, I tried honestly to empathize with each of them individually.

I write, as George Bernard Shaw said, for the same reason a cow gives milk: it's inside me, it's got to come out, and in a real sense I would die if I couldn't. It's the way I express my reaction to the world I live in. Sometimes the words come more easily than at other times, but writing is my lifeblood. *Riot* is my sixth book. But I have also pursued a United Nations career. I see myself as a human being with a number of responses to the world, some of which I manifest in my writing, some in my UN work (for refugees, in peace-keeping, in the secretary-general's office, and in communications). I think both writing and the UN are essential for my sanity: if I had given up either one, a part of my psyche would have withered on the vine.

I am often asked why, despite my international career, I have set all my books so far in India. The answer is simple. My formative years, from the ages of three to nineteen, were spent growing up in India. India shaped my mind, an-chored my identity, influenced my beliefs, and made me who I am. India matters immensely to me, and in all my writing, I would like to matter to India. Or, at least, to In-dian readers.

# 6

# Art for Heart's Sake

THE ONLY TIME I PROPERLY MET the incomparable Indian artist M. F. Husain (discounting, that is, the occasional fleeting handshakes in crowded gatherings) was in New York in 1993, over dinner at the home of the then Indian ambassador, Hamid Ansari. Sitting before the book-laden coffee table in the ambassador's Park Avenue living room, I recounted to the master the famous story of what the immortal Pablo Picasso used to say to aspiring artists of the avant-garde. Disregarding their slapdash cubes and squiggles, Picasso would demand: "Draw me a horse." Get the basics right, in other words, before you break free of them. Husain loved the story; he promptly opened the book in front of him, a volume of his own work from Ambassador Ansari's collection, and proceeded to sketch, with astonishing fluidity, a posse of horses on the frontispiece. I have never forgotten the moment: watching the artist's long brown fingers glide over the page, the horses' heads rearing, their manes flying, hooves and tails in the air, as Husain left, in a few bold strokes, the indelible imprint of his genius.

So to collaborate on a book with Husain was an extraordinary privilege. And to do so on the subject of my home state, Kerala, on which Husain had completed a series of astonishing paintings, made it a special pleasure as well.

For horses, in our volume, read elephants. They are everywhere in Husain's extraordinary evocation of Kerala: crashing through the dense foliage, embracing supple maidens with their trunks, and, in miniature, held aloft by triumphant womanhood. The elephants cavort by the waterside, drink, play, gambol, lurk. They are the animal form of the grandeur and gaiety of "God's Own Country." Elephants are indispensable to every Kerala celebration, from weddings to religious festivals; there is nothing in the world like the Thrissur Pooram, when hundreds emerge, bedecked with ornaments and flowers, to receive the homage of the Malayali people. Elephants infuse the Kerala consciousness; they feature in the state's literature, dance, music, films, and art. It is said that the true Keralite can tell one elephant apart from another just by looking at it. In their myriad shapes, sizes, and colors, Husain's elephants embody the magic of Kerala: the extraordinary natural beauty of the state, its lagoons, its forests, its beaches, and above all the startling, many-hued green of the countryside, with its emerald paddy fields and banana groves, and coconut and areca trees swaying in the gentle breeze that whispers its secrets across the land. And in their strength the elephants capture, too, the resilience of Kerala, its defiance of the Indian stereotype, its resolute determination to progress, and above all, its empowerment of women.

What can one say about this remarkable work and its remarkable subject, in this curious collaboration between a great artist who has signed his name in Malayalam, a language he cannot speak, and a writer who traces his roots to Kerala, a homeland he has only visited on his holidays? The "Marunaadan Malayali" — the expatriate Keralite — is so widespread, and so common, a phenomenon that the phrase has entered the Malayalam language. And here I am, one of the tribe, inspired by the paintings of a man who is the most "inside" of outsiders, seeking to capture in far too many words the insights into Kerala that he has illuminated with the dazzling fluency of his brush.

Though I am a Malayali and a writer, I have no claims to be considered a Malayali writer: indeed, despite setting some of my fictional sequences in Kerala and scattering several Menons through my stories, I could not have written my books in Malayalam because I cannot write my own mother tongue. And yet I am not inclined to be defensive about my Kerala heritage, despite the obvious incongruities of an expatriate praising Kerala from abroad and lauding the Malayali heritage in the English language.

As a child of the city, growing up in Bombay, Calcutta, and Delhi, my only experience of village Kerala had been as an initially reluctant vacationer during my parents' annual trips home. For many non-Keralite Malayali children traveling like this, there was often little joy in the compulsory rediscovery of their roots, and many saw it more as an obligation than a pleasure. For city-dwellers, rural Kerala (and Kerala is essentially rural, since the countryside envelops the towns in a seamless web) was a world of rustic simplicities and private inconveniences. When I was ten I told my father that this annual migration to the south was strictly for the birds. But as I grew older, I came to appreciate the magic of Kerala — its beauty, which Husain so exquisitely evokes, and also its ethos, which animates his images.

What does it mean, then, for Keralites like me, now living outside Kerala, to lay claim to our Malayali heritage? What is it of Kerala that we learn to cherish, and of which we remain proud, wherever we are? Those are the two questions I have tried to answer in my own essay accompanying Husain's paintings. In many ways my sense of Kerala is tied up with my sense of being Indian. I guess Husain could say something very similar himself. He has personalized my copy of our book not with horses or elephants, but with a boat, riding low in the water, taking us — like Kerala itself — gently forward.

# II

## Reconsiderations

# 7

# Right Ho, Sahib:
# Wodehouse and India

IT WAS AT THE HAY-ON-WYE FESTIVAL OF LITERATURE a few years ago that I realized with horror how low the fortunes of P. G. Wodehouse had sunk in his native land. I was on stage for a panel discussion on the works of the master when the moderator, a gifted and suave young literary impresario, began the proceedings by asking innocently, "So how do you pronounce it — is it Woad-house or Wood-house?"

Woadhouse? You could have knocked me over with the proverbial feather, except that Wodehouse himself would have disdained the cliché, instead describing my expression as, perhaps, that of one who "had swallowed an east wind" (*Carry On, Jeeves*, 1925). The fact was that a luminary at the premier book event in the British Isles — albeit one sponsored, it must be admitted, by the *Sunday Times* — had no idea how to pronounce the name of the man I regarded as the finest English writer since Shakespeare. I spent the rest of the panel discussion looking (to echo a description of Bertie Wooster's Uncle Tom) like a pterodactyl with a secret sorrow.

My dismay had Indian roots. Like many of my compatriots, I had discovered Wodehouse young and pursued my delight across the ninety-five volumes of the master's oeuvre, savoring book after book as if the pleasure would never end. When All India Radio announced, one sunny afternoon in February 1975, that P. G. Wodehouse had died, I felt a cloud of impenetrable darkness had settled over my day. The newly (and belatedly) knighted Sir Pelham Grenville Wodehouse, creator of Jeeves and of the prize pig the Empress of Blandings, was in his ninety-fourth year, but his death still came as a shock. Three decades earlier, Wodehouse had reacted to the passing of his stepdaughter, Leonora, with the numbed words: "I thought she was immortal." I had thought Wodehouse was immortal too, and I felt like one who had "drained the four-ale of life and found a dead mouse at the bottom of the pewter" (*Sam the Sudden*, also from that vintage year of 1925).

For months before his death I had procrastinated over a letter to Wodehouse. It was a collegian's fan letter, made special by being written on the letterhead (complete with curly-tailed pig) of the Wodehouse Society of St. Stephen's College, Delhi University. Ours was then the only Wodehouse society in the world, and I was its president, a distinction I prized over all others in an active and eclectic extracurricular life. The Wodehouse Society ran mimicry and comic speech contests and organized the annual Lord Ickenham Memorial Practical Joke Week, the bane of all at college who took themselves too seriously. The society's underground rag, *Spice*, edited by a wildly original classmate who was to go on to become a counselor to the prime minister of India, was by far the most popular newspaper on campus; even its misprints were deliberate, and deliberately funny.

I had wanted to tell the master all this, and to gladden his famously indulgent heart with the tribute being paid to him at this incongruous outpost of Wodehouseana thousands of miles away from any place he had ever written about. But I had never been satisfied by the prose of any of my drafts of the letter. Writing to the man Evelyn Waugh had called "the greatest living writer of the English language, the head of my profession" was like offering a soufflé to Bocuse. It had to be just right. Of course, it never was, and now I would never be able to reach out and establish this small connection to the writer who had given me more joy than anything else in my life.

The loss was personal, but it was also widely shared: P. G. Wodehouse was by far the most popular English-language writer in India, his readership exceeding that of Agatha Christie or Harold Robbins. His erudite butlers, absent-minded earls, and silly-ass aristocrats, out to pinch policemen's helmets on Boat Race Night or perform convoluted acts of petty larceny at the behest of tyrannical aunts, are familiar to, and beloved by, most educated Indians. I cannot think of an Indian family I know that does not have at least one Wodehouse book on its shelves, and most have several. In a country where most people's earning capacity has not kept up with international publishing inflation and book-borrowing is part of the culture, libraries stock multiple copies of each Wodehouse title. At the British Council libraries in the major Indian cities, demand for Wodehouse reputedly outstrips that for any other author, so that each month's list of "new arrivals" includes reissues of old Wodehouse favorites. Wodehouse's death was page-one news in every English-language newspaper in India; the articles and letters that were published in the following days about his life and work would have filled volumes.

In the three decades since his death, much has changed in India, but Wodehouse still commands the heights. His works are sold on railway station platforms and airport bookstalls alongside the latest best-sellers. In 1988 the state-run television network broadcast a ten-part Hindi adaptation of his 1923 classic *Leave It to Psmith*, with the Shropshire castle of the earl of Emsworth becoming the Rajasthani palace of an indolent maharaja. (The series was a disaster: Wodehousean purists were appalled by the changes, and the TV audience discovered that English humor does not translate too well into Hindi.) Quiz contests, a popular activity in urban India, continue to feature questions about Wodehouse's books ("What is Jeeves's first name?" "Which of Bertie Wooster's fiancées persisted in calling the stars 'God's daisy chain'?") But, alas, reports from St. Stephen's College tell me that the Wodehouse Society is now defunct, having fallen into disrepute when one of its Practical Joke Weeks went awry.

Many are astonished at the extent of Wodehouse's popularity in India, particularly when, elsewhere in the English-speaking world, he is no longer much read. Americans know Wodehouse from reruns of earlier TV versions of his short stories on programs with names like *Masterpiece Theatre* on public television, but these have a limited audience, even though some of Wodehouse's funniest stories were set in

Hollywood, and he lived the last three decades of his life in Remsenberg, Long Island. The critic Michael Dirda noted in the *Washington Post* some years ago that Wodehouse "seems to have lost his general audience and become mainly a cult author savored by connoisseurs for his prose artistry." That is increasingly true in England and the rest of the Commonwealth, but not in India. While no English-language writer can truly be said to have a "mass" following in India, where only 2 percent of the population read English, Wodehouse has maintained a general rather than a cult audience amongst this Anglophone minority: unlike others who have enjoyed fleeting success, he has never gone out of fashion. This bewilders those who think that nothing could be further removed from Indian life, with its poverty and political intensity, than the cheerfully silly escapades of Wodehouse's decadent Edwardian Young Men in Spats. Indians enjoying Wodehouse, they suggest, makes about as much sense as the cognoscenti of Chad lapping up Jay McInerney or Candace Bushnell.

At one level, India's fascination with Wodehouse is indeed one of those enduring and endearing international mysteries, like why Pakistanis are good at squash but none of their neighbors are, or why the Americans, who can afford to do anything correctly, have never managed to understand that tea is made with boiling water, not merely boiled water. And yet many have convinced themselves that there is more to it than that. Some have seen in Wodehouse's popularity a lingering nostalgia for the Raj, the British Empire in India. Writing in 1988, the journalist Richard West thought India's Wodehouse devotees were those who "hanker after the England of 50 years ago [i.e., the 1930s]. That was the age when the English loved and treasured their own language, when schoolchildren learned Shakespeare, Wordsworth and even Rudyard Kipling. . . . It was Malcolm Muggeridge who remarked that the Indians are now the last Englishmen. That may be why they love the quintessentially English writer, P. G. Wodehouse."

Those lines are, of course, somewhat more fatuous than anything Wodehouse himself ever wrote. Wodehouse is loved by Indians who loathe Kipling and detest the Raj and all its works. Indeed, despite a brief stint in a Hong Kong bank, Wodehouse had no colonial connection himself, and the Raj is largely absent from his books. (There is only one notable exception I can recall from his oeuvre, in a 1935 short story: "Why is there unrest in India? Because its inhabitants eat only an occasional handful of rice. The day when Mahatma Gandhi sits down to a good juicy steak and follows it up with roly-poly pudding and a spot of Stilton, you will see the end of all this nonsense of Civil Disobedience." But Indians saw that that comment was meant to elicit laughter, not agreement.) If anything, Wodehouse is one British writer whom Indian nationalists could admire without fear of political incorrectness. My former mother-in-law, the daughter of a prominent Indian nationalist politician, remembers introducing Britain's last viceroy, Lord Mountbatten, in 1947 to the works of Wodehouse; it was typical that the symbol of the British Empire had not read the "quintessentially English" Wodehouse but that the Indian freedom fighter had.

Indeed, it is precisely the lack of politics in Wodehouse's writing, or indeed of any other social or philosophical content, that made what Waugh called his "idyllic world" so free of the trappings of Englishness, quintessential or otherwise. Unlike almost any other writer, Wodehouse does not require his readers to identify with any of his characters: they are stock figures, almost theatrical archetypes whose carefully plotted exits and entrances one follows because they are amusing, not because one is actually meant to care about them. Whereas other English novelists burdened their readers with the specificities of their characters' lives and circumstances, Wodehouse's existed in a never-never land that was almost as unreal to his English readers as to his Indian ones. Indian readers were able to enjoy Wodehouse free of the anxiety of allegiance; for all its droll particularities, the world he created, from London's Drones Club to the village of Matcham Scratchings, was a world of the imagination, to which Indians required no visa.

But they did need a passport, and that was the English language. English was undoubtedly Britain's most valuable and abiding legacy to India, and educated Indians, a famously polyglot people, rapidly learned and delighted in it — both for itself, and as a means to various ends. These ends were both political (for Indians turned the language of the imperialists into the language of nationalism) and pleasurable (for the language granted access to a wider world of ideas and entertainments). It was only natural that Indians would enjoy a writer who used language as Wodehouse did — playing with its rich storehouse of classical precedents, mockingly subverting the very canons colonialism had taught Indians they were supposed to venerate. "He groaned slightly and winced, like Prometheus watching his vulture dropping in for lunch." Or: "The butler was looking nervous, like Macbeth interviewing Lady Macbeth after one of her visits to the spare room." And best of all, in a country ruled for the better part of two centuries by the dispensable siblings of the British nobility: "Unlike the male codfish which, suddenly finding itself the parent of three million five hundred thousand little codfish, cheerfully resolves to love them all, the British aristocracy is apt to look with a somewhat jaundiced eye on its younger sons."

That sentence captures much of the Wodehouse magic — what P. N. Furbank called his "comic pretence of verbal precision, an exhibition of lexicology." Wodehouse's writing embodied erudition, literary allusion, jocular slang, and an uncanny sense of timing that owed much to the long-extinct art of music-hall comedy: "She . . . [resembled] one of those engravings of the mistresses of Bourbon kings which make one feel that the monarchs who selected them must have been men of iron, impervious to fear, or else short-sighted." Furbank thought Wodehouse's "whole style [was] a joke about literacy." But it is a particularly literate joke. No authorial dedication will ever match Wodehouse's oft-plagiarized classic, for his 1925 collection of golfing stories *The Heart of a Goof*: "To my daughter Leonora, without whose never-failing sympathy and encouragement this book would have been finished in half the time."

Part of Wodehouse's appeal to Indians certainly lies in the uniqueness of his style, which inveigled us into a sort of conspiracy of universalism: his humor was inclusive, for his mock-serious generalizations were, of course, as absurd to those he was ostensibly writing about as to us. "Like so many substantial citizens of America, he had married young and kept on marrying, springing from blonde to blonde like the chamois of the Alps leaping from crag to crag." The terrifying Honoria Glossop has "a laugh like a squadron of cavalry charging over a tin bridge." Aunts, who always loom large in Wodehouse's world, bellow to each other "like mastodons across the primeval swamp." Jeeves, the gentleman's personal gentleman, coughs softly, like "a very old sheep clearing its throat on a distant mountain-top." Evelyn Waugh worshiped Wodehouse's penchant for tossing off original similes: "a soul as grey as a stevedore's undervest"; "her face was shining like the seat of a bus driver's trousers"; "a slow, pleasant voice, like clotted cream made audible"; "she looked like a tomato struggling for self-expression." My own favorites stretch the possibilities of the language in unexpected ways: "She had more curves than a scenic railway"; "I turned him down like a bedspread"; and the much-quoted "if not actually disgruntled, he was far from being gruntled."

This insidious but good-humored subversion of the language, conducted with straight-faced aplomb, appeals most of all to a people who have acquired English but rebel against its heritage. The colonial connection left strange patterns on the minds of the connected. Wodehouse's is a world we can share with the English on equal terms, because they are just as surprised by its enchantments. As we celebrate the hundredth anniversary of the publication of his first novel, perhaps that is as good an argument as any for a long-overdue Wodehouse revival in England.

# 8

# The Last Englishman: Malcolm Muggeridge

DURING 2003, A GREAT DEAL, SOME OF IT VALUABLE, was written about the much-heralded centenary of that great writer and humanist George Orwell. But earlier that year most of the world press missed another centenary altogether — also that of an Englishman of letters with something of an Indian connection. This might not be entirely surprising, since few reputations are as evanescent as those forged in the transient arena of popular journalism, which is where Malcolm Muggeridge, who would have turned one hundred in March 2003, made his name. But just three decades ago, at the height of his fame, Malcolm Muggeridge was surely among the half-dozen best-known Britons in India, and it is a little too soon, in my view, for us to have completely forgotten him.

Muggeridge is best remembered in India as the man who "discovered" Mother Teresa — the journalist whose impassioned reporting of her work, captured first on BBC television and then more memorably in the 1969 book

*Something Beautiful for God,* first catapulted the Calcutta missionary to worldwide attention. At the time Muggeridge declared that he "saw life as an eternal battle between two irreconcilable opposites, the world of the flesh and the world of the spirit." His admiration for Mother Teresa helped convince him of the triumph of the spirit, and turned him into an increasingly religious figure, who was finally received into the Roman Catholic faith in 1982, at the age of seventy-nine. "God made the world," Muggeridge observed, "and saw that it was good." When he died in 1990 it was the Malcolm Muggeridge of Catholic compassion whom the Indian obituarists all memorialized.

But this was in fact an unlikely ending for a notorious libertine; for most of his life it was the world of the flesh that Muggeridge inhabited, and in which he dazzled. The son of a socialist factory clerk in a London suburb, Malcolm Muggeridge was a brilliant student at Cambridge who developed by his late twenties into a formidable writer and commentator of sharp intelligence, admirable originality ("never forget that only dead fish swim with the stream," he once remarked), and coruscating wit (Prime Minister Anthony Eden "was not only a bore, he bored for England"). Muggeridge wrote plays, published novels, and reported on pretty much every event of worldwide importance from the 1930s to the 1970s. He did so, of course, in print, his byline appearing in virtually every English newspaper we have ever heard of in India, from the *Guardian* and the *New Statesman* to the *Listener* and *Punch* (which he edited for five years). But he was also a famous radio broadcaster on the BBC from the 1940s, and an early television celebrity, so famous in Britain that Madame Tussaud's immortalized him in wax in 1968 alongside such other cultural icons of the day as Elizabeth Taylor and the Beatles.

Muggeridge also produced a remarkable amount of personal reflection, scribbling frank and perceptive dissections of his contemporaries into his diaries (for the delectation thereafter of a wide readership), and authoring two volumes of memoirs with the delicious title *Chronicles of Wasted Time.* Much of Muggeridge's appeal, it must be said, lay in his irreverence. Visiting Tokyo after World War II, he attended a public appearance by Emperor Hirohito and described him as a "nervous, shy, stuttering, pathetic figure, formerly god." He began an interview with Salvador Dalí not with some pretentious question about modern art but by asking what happened to the painter's famous upwardly pointed mustaches at night ("they droop," Dalí replied). Muggeridge was so contemptuous of the soap-opera conduct of the British royal family in the 1950s that the BBC briefly exiled him from the ether (he was too popular for them to banish him altogether). This was in reaction to the relatively decorous affair between Princess Margaret and the gentlemanly Group Captain Peter Townsend; one shudders to think what Muggeridge would have made of Princess Di and Fergie.

But if he was famously contrarian, it was in the service of a larger cause — the preservation of a society in which "everything should be subject to criticism," authority was always suspect, and conformism was to be avoided. Though brought up as a socialist, and married to the niece of the famous Fabians Sidney and Beatrice Webb, Muggeridge was wary of the socialists' starry-eyed idealism, and fierce in his denunciations of Stalinism. Reporting from Moscow, he was amongst the first to broadcast exposés of Soviet tyranny, at a time when the Communist experiment was still idealized by the Left; and he was equally early to denounce Fascism and Nazism in his journalism from Berlin. Within a decade of World War II he was scathing about the dangers of liberalism, calling it "the destructive force of the age" because it assumed a willingness on the part of individuals to live amicably "seeking one another's good" — a "fantasy" that "in human terms, cannot be." Hence Muggeridge on the welfare state: "a kind of zoo which provides its inmates with ease and comfort and unfits them for life in their natural habitat."

It is clearly a long way from such robustly individualist views to the softly glowing halo Muggeridge placed on Mother Teresa. A chain-smoking, hard-drinking philanderer who was notorious for his advances to every passing woman (and whose own wife matched him in the frequency and variety of her adulteries), Muggeridge seems an unlikely convert to religious faith, let alone one as rigorous and doctrinaire as Catholicism. "His enemies, and even his friends," according to the critic Roger Kimball, "saw in him the aging reprobate who, stymied by flagging appetite, rails against the sins of his youth and cravenly turns to religion." Many would prefer to remember the Muggeridge who, when told on TV by the preacher Billy Graham that only God could answer one of his questions, responded tartly: "And we haven't got Him in the studio — or," he added, rolling his eyes to the ceiling, "have we?"

Malcolm Muggeridge is largely forgotten today, but his life is not his only legacy. "From earliest childhood," Muggeridge once recalled, "it always seemed to me that the only thing worth doing in life was to write." What words will endure no writer can know, but for those of us who have to struggle to find the time to write, that motto remains an inspiration.

# 9

# Blood and Bombast:
# Winston Churchill

I<small>T IS POSSIBLE, I HAVE RECENTLY DISCOVERED,</small> to admire a biographer even when one dislikes the subject of an admiring biography. Having met and spoken with Roy Jenkins, the octogenarian parliamentarian best known in India for splitting the British Labour Party in the 1970s in the name of social democracy, I feel doubly admiring of his massive, 1002-page biography of that overweening imperialist, Winston Churchill.

Jenkins, an active Liberal Democratic peer in the House of Lords until his death in 2003, was unusually well qualified to write a biography of Winston Churchill. Both were politicians whose convictions triumphed over party loyalty; both dedicated their remarkable intellects to a combination of politics and literature; both earned superb reputations as parliamentarians, leavened by a well-advertised fondness for the good life (burgundy was to Jenkins what champagne and brandy were for Churchill); and both served the crown as home secretary and as chancellor of the exchequer. That

Churchill was on the right of British politics and Jenkins on the left does not seem to have impeded the biographer's enthusiasm, though Jenkins takes care to construct a case that Churchill was no mere aristocratic conservative: he "was far too many-faceted, idiosyncratic and unpredictable a character to allow himself to be imprisoned by the circumstances of his birth. His devotion to his career [was] . . . far stronger than any class or tribal loyalty."

Both also, it must be said, have a remarkable gift for words, and the biographer's style is fully worthy of his famous subject. Jenkins first, since we have all heard much more of Churchill: on Churchill's father, Randolph, he writes, "He had the gift of insolence, which can be defined as the ability to think up memorably amusing phrases and the nerve to deliver them without fear." Jenkins is not much kinder to Winston's other parent, his notoriously promiscuous American mother, Jennie: "George Moore, the Anglo-Irish novelist, said she had 200 lovers, but apart from anything else the number is suspiciously round."

This tone of learned but irreverent wit is undoubtedly in keeping with his subject, for few historical figures have been as defined by their use of language as Winston Churchill. Churchill's reputation as what Harold Evans has called "the British Lionheart on the ramparts of civilization" rests almost entirely on his stirring rhetoric during World War II. Churchill had nothing to offer but "blood, toil, tears and sweat." And, of course, an exceptional talent for a fine phrase. "We shall not flag nor fail. We shall go on to the end. . . . We shall fight them on the beaches, we shall fight them on the landing grounds, we shall fight them in the

BLOOD AND BOMBAST: WINSTON CHURCHILL

fields and in the streets. . . . We shall never surrender."
(The revisionist British historian John Charmley dismissed
this as "sublime nonsense.") Churchill never flinched from
bombast: "Let us therefore brace ourselves to our duties,
and so bear ourselves that if the British Empire and its
Commonwealth last for a thousand years, men will still say,
'This was their finest hour.'" Such extravagant oratory helped
steel the British at a time of great adversity, but its effect
was only of the moment. Yet Churchill believed that "words
are the only things which last forever." The hagiology from
which he has benefited in the last fifty years suggests that
he may well have been right.

And what words they were! "You ask, what is our policy? I will say: It is to wage war, by sea, land and air, with all
our might and with all the strength that God can give us. . . .
You ask, what is our aim? I can answer in one word: It is victory, victory at all costs, victory in spite of all terror, victory,
however long and hard the road may be; for without victory,
there is no survival." That victory, as Charmley has pointed
out, resulted in the dissolution of the British Empire and,
more immediately, in Churchill's own defenestration by the
war-weary British electorate in the elections of 1945. But
Churchill cheerfully said that history would judge him kindly
because he intended to write it himself. (The vaingloriously
self-serving but elegant volumes he authored on the war led
the Nobel Committee, unable in all conscience to give him
an award for peace, to give him, astonishingly enough, the
Nobel Prize for Literature — an unwitting tribute to the fictional qualities inherent in Churchill's self-justifying em-
bellishments.)

To be fair to Jenkins, his authoritatively researched, marvelously written tome goes well beyond the words to paint an inspired portrait of the man who straddled the great events of the late nineteenth and early twentieth centuries. Here is Churchill the cavalryman of the Boer War and the Sudan campaign, Churchill the defiant bulldog who kept the British in World War II when so many of the establishment wanted peace, and Churchill the parliamentarian of rapier wit who dominated its politics at a time when Britain was the epicenter of a worldwide empire. At the end of his research, Jenkins, a highly regarded biographer of Herbert Henry Asquith and William E. Gladstone, concludes: "When I started writing this book I thought that Gladstone was, by a narrow margin, the greater man, certainly the more remarkable specimen of humanity. In the course of writing it I changed my mind. I now put Churchill, with all his idiosyncrasies, his indulgences, his occasional childishness, but also his genius, his tenacity and his persistent ability, right or wrong, successful or unsuccessful, to be larger than life, as the greatest human being ever to occupy 10 Downing Street."

I do think that Jenkins makes the best case that can be made for this conclusion, but he conceded, when I asked him directly, that Churchill's greatness was deeply flawed by two major failings. One was his disastrous judgment on military matters, going back to the horrendous defeat at Gallipoli in 1915, a plan he hatched when first lord of the Admiralty, and reflected again in Norway in 1940, as well as in his decision to delay the planned 1943 invasion of Europe in favor of a pointless diversionary campaign in North Africa in 1942 (which in turn led inevitably to the great Allied losses in Italy, where the topography overwhelmingly favored the defenders). Jenkins addresses these errors unsparingly. The second major failing, which Jenkins does not adequately address in his book, was that Churchill's notions of freedom and democracy, his defense of which led *Time* magazine to hail him as the "Man of the Century," faltered at the frontiers of empire. My blood still boils when I hear teary-eyed British friends describe him as a great fighter for freedom, when I know him principally as a blinkered imperialist untroubled by the oppression of nonwhite peoples, a man who fought to deny us freedom. (And he did so with a pettiness that cannot be excused on grounds of policy: after presiding over one of the worst famines in human history, the Great Bengal Famine of 1943, while ordering the diversion of food from starving civilians to well-supplied Tommies, Churchill's only response to a telegram from the government in Delhi about the people perishing in the famine was to ask peevishly why Gandhi hadn't died yet.)

That story is not told in the Jenkins book; nor are the numerous other tales of Churchill's supremacist bigotry. When I asked Jenkins about this, his answer was honest: Churchill, he admitted bluntly, "was a racialist." It is, alas, a judgment that does not figure in the book, but Lord Jenkins's candor and willingness to qualify his own admiration of his subject is testimony to his intellectual integrity. In his egotistical, arrogant, and unsympathetic inability to rise above the crippling prejudices of the worst of his race, Churchill was a lesser man than his biographer.

# 10

# The Spy Who Stayed Out in the Cold

O F THE MANY UNPREDICTABLE, AND SOMETIMES CALAMI-
TOUS, consequences of the end of the Cold War, the
one with the most impact on the world's readers has been
the sudden collapse of the rich lode mined for four decades
by the world's spy novelists. The shadowy, sinister, and oc-
casionally explosive shenanigans of secret agents contending on the margins of the superpower standoff provided
page-turning grist to many a literary mill. Entire reputations
were built on Cold War fiction. When the Berlin Wall fell,
one of the more anxious questions that arose amid the rubble
was, "What will John Le Carré write about now?"

*The Night Manager* and *The Secret Pilgrim* provided part
of the answer, but they were still in the genre, a coda to the
last kick of the cold warriors. Le Carré's next novel, *Our
Game,* offered a more conclusive response. Not only was it
Le Carré's first truly post–Cold War book, but its release was
accompanied by a flurry of nonfiction articles and interviews
in which the author explicitly spelled out his own view of

the new world order. The presumed distance between narrative fiction and the politics of the narrator has thus been eliminated. *Our Game* is about Le Carré's game, what one might call his new word order. And that is both its most intriguing feature and its most crippling handicap.

Timothy Cranmer, Le Carré's protagonist, is a retired British counterespionage agent living in sybaritic luxury in the Somerset countryside with a beautiful young musician, Emma Manzini. The end of the Cold War has made him surplus to requirements, as it has the "joe" he used to run as a double agent, Larry Pettifer. Larry, an agent of passion and reckless charm, is now a professor at Bath University, giving lectures on such subjects as "The Squandered Victory: Western Foreign Policy since 1988." At the novel's beginning, Larry has disappeared; so, we soon discover, has Emma, whom Cranmer had reluctantly introduced to the irresistible Larry.

The plot thickens like Yeltsin's waistline, and at the time of Le Carré's writing, it was just as topical. Larry's old KGB contact Checheyev, a Muslim from the southern Russian republic of Ingushetia in the northern Caucasus, has milked his ex-Soviet employers of $37 million and is apparently using it, with Larry's help, to acquire arms to finance an Ingush rebellion against Moscow. Cranmer, suspected by his former colleagues of involvement in Larry's misdeeds, sets out to find his friend and his ex-lover, a journey that returns him to the spy's life of death and double-dealing.

At one level, the device of Cranmer's quest for Larry and Emma keeps the pages turning, drawing the reader into the chase that is a classic staple of the genre. But Cranmer is a

maddeningly elusive spy-hero: he cannot remember whether
he has killed Larry in a fight, he cannot guess what the
money might have been stolen for, he stretches out deduc-
tions he might have made much earlier from clues already
in his possession. When is a thriller not a thriller? In this
case, when it has no surprises, when it eschews action, when
it even sidesteps a climactic battle toward which it seems to
have been building, and when its principal leitmotif is not
the gripping yarn of the blurbs but a political harangue from
the op-ed pages.

For it was, in fact, in a philippic in the *New York Times*
op-ed page the previous December that Le Carré nailed his
colors to the mast: "Having won the cold war, the West can't
afford to walk away from the consequences of its victory:
whether we are speaking of Bosnia today, Chechnya or Ingushetia tomorrow or Cuba the day after." His fierce assault
on the West's current policy toward Russia was followed by
an article in the *New York Times Book Review* describing the
spirit in which he had embarked on this novel. "The West,
it seemed to me, had dishonored every pledge we had made
during the Cold War. We continued to protect the strong
against the weak. When small nations were butchered, the
best we could manage was the tutting of an anxious by-
stander."

Compare this to what the narrator defensively describes
as Larry's "turgid expositions" about his political choice: "It
happens to be the Ingush because they exemplify everything most shabby about our post–Cold War world." Instead
of "defend[ing] the underdog against the bully . . . the West
made common cause with the bully in favor of what we call

stability." Larry goes on: "The Ingush refuse . . . to be ignored, devalued or dismissed. And what they are fighting against . . . is a whorehouse alliance between a rotten Russian Empire marching to its old tunes and a Western leadership that in its dealings with the rest of the world has proclaimed moral indifference to be its decent Christian right."

Back to Le Carré: "I picked on the North Caucasus for the setting of my novel because . . . I wanted to say something bitter about the repression of small nations, and about the unfashionable wars that politicians may safely ignore." This thesis animates the novel: Cranmer's search for Larry is that of the soulless professional looking for the idealist of principle. "I don't think you wish to find your friend, only to become him," a minor character (inserted, it seems, only to utter that line) tells Cranmer. If and when the Ingush are crushed, Checheyev says to Cranmer, "part of you will die. Because what we have is what you used to fight for when you were men." It is hardly surprising that Cranmer soon "begged to be allowed to take the Caucasus into my protection."

Ever since *The Spy Who Came in from the Cold* nearly three decades ago, I had thought of John Le Carré as the author who had deromanticized the spy novel. He had created a grim and gray world of petty routine and grand betrayal, a world so gloomy its chief protagonist preferred to die on the Berlin Wall than to continue its amoral battles. With *Our Game*, a title deliberately reminiscent of the "Great Game" that the British imperialists of a century ago thought they were playing against czarist Russia, it is clear that Le Carré has made of disillusionment merely another kind of romanticism.

And sure enough, Cranmer says of Larry, "What

powered him . . . was his romanticism, his love of the underdog, his gut contempt for the British Establishment and
its crawling adherence to America. Larry's hatreds didn't
change when Communism collapsed. Neither did his loves.
His dreams of a better, fairer world didn't change — his love
of the individuality over the collective. . . . After the Cold
War it got worse. On both sides of the Atlantic. More corrupt, inward, conformist, intolerant, isolationist, smug. . . .
Why shouldn't Larry continue to betray us?"

Le Carré's own hatreds and loves haven't changed either. In an excoriating account of an encounter with the former KGB general Oleg Kalugin, he has written, "To listen
to him you could be forgiven for assuming that we had been
on the same side all along." Le Carré has no doubt which
side he remains on. He is contemptuous of today's Russo-
American entente, whereby (in words from the novel that
echo those of his op-ed) "whatever Moscow does is O.K. by
Washington, provided nobody frightens the horses. End of
policy." It is symbolic of this not-so-brave new world that
Cranmer discovers that "the Office," as he calls it, has been
relocated after his retirement in "a sullen multistory block-
house, rooted amid tearing traffic, all-night cafes, and down-
at-heel clothing shops." A far cry from the days when spies
were spies and God was a Russian-hating Englishman.

The irony is that Le Carré the author is guilty of the
very sin he also ascribes to Western policy makers, that of
"hunt[ing] wistfully for a new means of dividing the world
for our greater comfort and safety, now that the Communist
thing, rather regrettably, had gone away." In conjuring up a
world where a postimperial monster state is bent on subju-

gating fiercely individualist little republics as the West stands cynically (or cravenly) by, he has perpetuated an old division, one based on the continuing demonization of the old enemy, Russia. And so the Ingush are romanticized: "We're a bunch of unruly mountaineers who love God, drink, fight, boast, steal, forge a little money, push a little gold, wage blood feuds, and can't be organized into groups of more than one."

In this post–Cold War world, to paraphrase an old joke from the novel, there will be no big war, but in the struggle for peace not a stone will be left standing. Spy novelists may well need to encourage passionate insurrections to give themselves, and their characters, new moral causes to struggle for. But for the rest of us, wary of the endless multiplication of sovereignties, hesitant before the clamor for self-determination echoing in a hundred different dialects, anxious about murderous new fundamentalisms, and unconvinced that any part of the old Soviet Union really needs another Englishman "to take the Caucasus into [his] protection," perhaps it would be better if those stones were left standing after all. In which case Le Carré's indignation seems overblown and the political message of his fiction, for all the elegance of its writing and the smooth flow of its prose, a somewhat disingenuous and self-defeating exercise.

Having failed to revive the Cold War, Le Carré turned his attentions to the developing world, with a similarly dystopic vision. His next novel, *The Tailor of Panama*, the story of an unfortunate seamster who is blackmailed into becoming a British agent, soon had all of Panama up in arms — though, fortunately for the author, not literally.

Le Carré, apparently requiring more than just a spy story in these days when the life and death of a secret agent has few earthshaking consequences, produced a particularly nasty portrait of the Central American country, one describing it entirely as a land of corruption and betrayal. "There's no hope for us," one of his Panamanian characters says. "What do we do? Cheat. Conspire. Lie. Pretend. Steal. Starve each other. . . . We're so stupid and corrupt and blind I don't know why the earth doesn't swallow us up right now."

It gets worse. Those on both sides of Panama's more famous earth opening, the canal, reacted with fury to this "national insult." For it seems that most of the book's characters, from the president on down, are so thinly disguised as to be instantly recognizable as real Panamanians, including many who offered Le Carré a hospitable welcome on his research visit. "Ugly, unreal and unjust" is one alliterative condemnation; another compared Le Carré's book to a portrait of America based purely on the deeds of Al Capone.

This is, no doubt, all good fun, if you don't happen to be Panamanian. It is even possible that Le Carré's research was more accurate than, say, that of Paul Mann, who has built a formidable award-winning reputation in the Western world for thrillers set in an India so grotesque, so revolting, and so replete with howlers that only a non-Indian could read them without his blood boiling over. What bothers me about the likes of Mann is that, to sell their tawdry tales of fetid exotica, they pretend to be portraying an entire society, peddling their hollow knowingness as if it were insight. I do not know enough about Panama to judge whether Le Carré is guilty of the same sin, but the problem is a familiar one.

In Le Carré's case the dilemma is existential. In our post–Cold War world, his Great Cause has disappeared. So Le Carré dressed up a petty cause as a great one, buttressing his feeble fictions with op-ed assaults on the post–Cold War peace between the superpowers. His novels, he admitted, served to abet his assault on the West's new entente with Russia; he is the spy who never came in from the cold. Maybe, just maybe, Le Carré should stick to writing about the gray and gloomy England he knows best, rather than trying to set to rights a world that has moved beyond the sterile divisions of a global antagonism that threatened us all.

# 11

# Remembering Pushkin

IT IS A MEASURE OF THE EXTENT to which colonialism has shaped our perception of the world that Indians know so little of the work of the greatest Russian poet, Alexander Pushkin, the two-hundredth anniversary of whose birth was celebrated as the last millennium was ending.

Innumerable British poets of flimsy attainment have entered our imaginations and our schoolbooks, but Pushkin remains a closed book to us. Literate Indians can quote from "The Solitude of Alexander Selkirk" and turn misty-eyed at yet another recitation of "Casabianca," with its boy standing on the burning deck, but ask us to name one of Pushkin's masterworks, and we are lost. All three poets flourished at roughly the same time — the late eighteenth/early nineteenth century — but neither Selkirk's creator, William Cowper, nor the very English Felicia Hemans, whose faithful boy went down on his ship the *Casabianca*, have any international literary stature today. Pushkin, on the other hand, is not just immortal: he is recognized as the creator of modern Russian language and literature, no less, and as the writer who has captured the Russian soul as no other writer has before or since.

Yet — pick up the *Penguin Dictionary of Quotations*, that hallmark of British literary recognition, and you will find six pages devoted to Cowper: a staggering 147 quotations. Even the deservedly obscure Hemans gets seven listings. And Pushkin? Not even one. He doesn't appear at all. It's not just because he's "foreign," since the *Penguin Dictionary*, with admirable eclecticism, has quotes from Goethe and Heine, Ibsen and Voltaire. It's just that the Anglocentric view of the world has never had much room for Pushkin.

But just listen to Russians about this man! Aleksandr Sergeyevich Pushkin, an exotic nobleman whose maternal great-grandfather, a black African, came to Russia in the days of Peter the Great, embodies the Russian spirit as no purely Caucasian writer ever has. He died in a futile duel at the tragically young age of thirty-eight and yet wrote lines that were memorized by czars and Communists alike. Listen to the woman in a Moscow bookstore who told a Western journalist, "Pushkin is my spirit, he is my soul." Heed the twentieth-century Russian poet who declared that "Pushkin is our everything."

Pushkin's was an extraordinary life by any measure. By twenty-one, he had published his first major poem, "Ruslan and Ludmila," a courageous "Ode to Liberty," and a clutch of satirical poems that so offended the czar that he was promptly exiled from Saint Petersburg to southern Russia. Banishment didn't cramp his literary style, and he produced the hugely popular epic poem "The Prisoner of the Caucasus."

The court, mindful of his fame, ordered him back to his family's luxurious estate, Mikhailovskoye — a sort of genteel house arrest — and two years later pardoned him. Pushkin settled first in Moscow and then in Saint Petersburg, producing the book-length verse-novel *Yevgeny Onegin*, a masterpiece that is revered as one of the greatest works of Russian literature, was adapted as an opera by Tchaikovsky, and even inspired India's own Vikram Seth, in San Francisco, to write his novel in verse, *The Golden Gate*.

There followed a flurry of other great works, including the novel *The Captain's Daughter* and most notably *Boris Godunov*, a verse drama that was the basis for Modest Mussorgsky's most famous opera and also for an award-winning Soviet film. Pushkin was working on a novel about his African ancestor — titled *The Negro of Peter the Great* — when a duel sparked by his unhappy marriage ended his short and brilliant life.

Pushkin revolutionized Russian literature, deriving images and themes from his country's history and folklore and using contemporary language shunned by traditional writers. His impact on his country's cultural self-perception simply cannot be overestimated: it is far greater than Goethe's in Germany, comparable only to Rabindranath Tagore's in Bengal. To be fair, Pushkin, rather like Tagore, has proved difficult to translate. The Russian scholar Valentin Nepomnyaschy explains it well: "Of the world's [literary] geniuses, he is least translated into other languages and the hardest to grasp in translation: in cultures with other languages, he seizes the soul only of those who know and love our language, our culture, those to whom Russia is not spiritually alien."

Russia is indeed spiritually alien to the world outside Eastern Europe; still, our ignorance of Pushkin is shocking. But it is not entirely surprising. For all English speakers in India are products of a colonial education, the legacy of Thomas Babington Macaulay and his self-satisfied successors. We have internalized a literary value system that emerged from the British desire to teach their literature as an instrument of their imperial domination. Let the natives admire our great works, the assumption ran, and they will admire our rule as well; a babu shaken by Shakespeare will also be charmed by Churchill. What Indian would defy Dufferin who has been awed by Defoe?

To their credit, the British were right for a long time. But it took the supremely well-read and cultured Jawaharlal Nehru to see beyond the worldview the British offered their colonial subjects. Today, after five and a half decades of independence, a perusal of India's literary pages shows that his intellectual legatees have a wider literary horizon: Shakespeare and Eliot, certainly, but also Goethe and García Márquez, Kundera and Kenzaburo Oe. But though it is never too late to discover a great writer, it remains a standing reproach to India's proliferating publishers that there is practically no available translation of Pushkin.

# 12

# The Committed Poet

THE CENTENARY OF THE BIRTH of the great Chilean poet
Pablo Neruda, on July 12, 2004, has passed, but how
can any writer allow it to pass unremarked? It is not merely
the Nobel Prize for Literature that he won in 1971 that
marks Neruda as one of the greatest literary figures of the
last century. It is surely the extent to which his life and his
poetry lives on in the souls of readers everywhere — most
particularly in the Spanish-speaking world, but also, thanks
to some excellent translations, across the globe as well.
Neruda's poetry illuminates the Spanish language, its lines
cited, its sentiments absorbed, to a greater extent than, say,
Eliot's in English. His passion, his rage, his tenderness, his
wit, are as familiar and beloved to literate Hispanics as Rabindranath Tagore's to Bengalis. And unlike most poets,
Neruda was a man of action, serving his country as a diplomat and politician, always willing to put his life and limb at
the service of his convictions.

The combination gave him a following few writers

have ever known in their lifetimes. One of my favorite stories of Neruda is of the time in his early sixties when he was addressing an audience in a Latin American country and was asked by a fan to recite a particular poem. Neruda started doing so, and faltered; the poem had been written many years earlier, and his own memory was no longer so reliable. As the aging poet stood on the stage, stumbling for his half-forgotten words, a man rose from the audience and recited the next line. Then another got up to join him, and another; and soon the entire audience was on its feet, reciting the poem, as its author stood silent and humbled, listening to his poetry coming back to him through the voices — and the hearts — of his readers.

Neruda, the son of a railroad worker, published his first poem at thirteen. He was only sixteen — an age when many of us are barely growing out of short pants — when he decided that the name he was born with (Ricardo Eliecer Neftali Reyes Basoalto) would not do for him. He chose, instead, to rename himself Pablo (a simple Spanish name already being made famous by the great painter Picasso) Neruda (after the Czech writer Jan Neruda, whom he greatly admired). Within four years he had already published a book of poetry that stunned the world: *Twenty Love Poems and a Song of Despair*. Eight decades of lovers since then have romanced each other with lines written by a twenty-year-old. Twenty-nine more volumes were to follow, though Pablo Neruda entered his country's diplomatic service (poetry has never been a generous paymaster). From love, to an evocative humanism in *Residence on Earth* (1933), through the powerful and deceptively simple *Elementary Odes* (1958),

Neruda sparkled with a brilliance that was both fierce and memorable.

He was, it must be said, a writer "engagé." His politics was not merely leftist; he was a committed Communist and — though it seems awkward to admit it today, after all we know of the Soviet strongman's cruelties — avowedly Stalinist. His political convictions were really forged (like those of so many others at that time) in the crucible of the Spanish Civil War. Neruda had, after minor consular posts in Asia and Argentina, been assigned to Spain in 1934, just as tensions between the Republicans and the Fascists were beginning to reach boiling point. His postings in places like Colombo and Rangoon had already awakened his consciousness of the perverse iniquities of colonialism, and he had even been boycotted by British society in Burma for his heretical views. ("The boycott," he wrote, "couldn't have pleased me more. Those intolerant Europeans were not really interesting. . . . I had not come to the Orient to spend my life with transient colonizers but with the ancient spirit of that world.") When his friend, the great Spanish poet Federico Lorca, was murdered by the Fascists in August 1936, Neruda crossed the Rubicon. Not only did he write his classic poem about the war, "Spain in My Heart," but he intervened to save the lives of some two thousand leftist refugees by transporting them by sea to Chile. Neruda's official role in the evacuation as a diplomat was matched by his passionate self-justification in his poetry. In a powerful poem, "Let Me Explain a Few Things," Neruda traced his own change from the romantic who had authored love poems to the committed righter of the world's wrongs: "You will ask why his poetry / does not speak of dreams and leaves?" he wrote. And then he provided the ringing answer: "Come and see the blood in the streets / Come and see the blood in the streets!"

Diplomacy was clearly not going to be enough for someone with such a seething passion for justice, and Neruda resigned his diplomatic position as Chilean consul-general in Mexico City in 1940. He delighted in returning home. "I believe a man should live in his own country," he wrote in his memoirs. "I think the deracination of human beings leads to frustration in one way or another, obstructing the light of the soul." Having given up diplomacy he entered politics, being elected as a senator in 1945, the year he also formally joined the Communist Party. Even those of us who see little to commend in communism as an ideology or the Communist Party as an institution cannot fail to be moved by the direct simplicity of his poem "To My Party." Far from the jargon-laden propaganda of the usual Marxist tracts, Neruda's poem soars in its vision: "You have given me brotherhood towards the man I do not know. / You have given me the added strength of all those living. . . . / You showed me how one person's pain could die in the victory of all. . . . / You have made me indestructible, for I no longer end in myself." Through Neruda's magnificent words, it is easier to understand how so many young idealists at the time found inspiration in Communist solidarity.

A clash with Chile's tyrannical rulers was inevitable. After a passionate denunciation of the government in a Venezuelan newspaper (no Chilean paper was prepared to publish it) was followed by a courageous speech in the Senate accusing the authorities of running a concentration camp, Neruda was forced to go into hiding in 1948. He lived underground, protected by friends, for a year before fleeing Chile in disguise in a bold horseback ride across the mountains to Argentina, during which he nearly perished. He made it after a couple of harrowing episodes, carrying with him a precious manuscript of poems, *Canto General*. There followed three years of exile in Europe (part of which was recently immortalized in the marvelous Italian film *The Postman*, though it omitted his once having to escape arrest by fleeing on a gondola in Venice).

On his return to Chile, Neruda remained active politically and was even nominated for the presidency of his country. He stepped aside for his friend Salvador Allende, who was finally elected in 1970 and named Neruda his ambassador to France. Ill health prompted the poet-diplomat to return home in late 1972. It was there that Neruda followed in anguish the coup that toppled Allende's government. As a prominent Communist, Neruda was raided by the military on his deathbed, but was spirited enough to say to the commander who marched into his bedroom: "There is only one thing of danger for you here — my poetry!"

Twelve days after the fall of the Allende government, Pablo Neruda died. His body lay for two days in his house, which had been ransacked by soldiers, and his funeral became the occasion for perhaps the only spontaneous popular demonstration against the military dictatorship. In his memorable poem "The Heights of Machu Picchu" he had written of the permanence of that durable Inca rock fortress ("the rock that abides, and the word"), but now it would be of Neruda himself that the next lines spoke: "death's plenitude holding us here, a bastion, the fullness / of life like a blow falling." In his poem "The Poet's Obligation" Neruda had declared: "To whoever is not listening to the sea / this Friday morning, to whoever is cooped up / in house or office, factory or woman / or street or mine or dry prison cell, / to him I come, and without speaking or looking / I arrive and open the door of his prison."

Those prison doors will always remain open to anyone who can pick up a volume of Neruda's. His biographer Adam Feinstein recounts how one morning soon after his death there was an uproar in a house where Neruda had used to live — a huge eagle had gotten into the living room, though all the doors and windows of the house had been locked for months. Pablo Neruda had always said that in his next life he wanted to be an eagle. No doubt his wish was fulfilled, and he soars above us today, like his poetry.

# 13

# Speaking Ill of the Dead:
# Nirad Chaudhuri

ONE MUST NEVER SPEAK ILL OF THE DEAD, of course, though it is tempting to wonder whether that old dictum applies to those who themselves, while they were alive, reveled in speaking ill of both the dead and the living. Still, now that the eulogies for the late Nirad Chaudhuri, who died in 1999, have been heard and read and no doubt filed away, only to be exhumed at the next unsuitable opportunity, one wonders whether the traditional kindness to the departed soul colored rather too much of our judgment.

From the publication of his *Autobiography of an Unknown Indian* shortly after Independence through a series of disquisitions on his native India and the Britain to which he emigrated, Nirad Chaudhuri acquired a formidable reputation as a stylist and a contrarian. In books with arch titles like *Thy Hand, Great Anarch!* Chaudhuri placed his considerable erudition and florid English at the service of a worldview that combined personal introspection with ethnic self-hatred. It did not help that, though he was born in 1897, his political sensibilities seemed grounded in the nineteenth century; certainly his education, whether formal or self-taught, appears to have taken little account of ideas elaborated since then. British critics found in him an Indian they could agree with, and painlessly admire; the Indians who frothed at the mouth at his reactionary views were dismissed by Chaudhuri with the contempt that he reserved for most of his compatriots.

The conventional wisdom — at least as reflected in the generous sampling of elegiac obituaries I read — is that Nirad-babu, as he was known in the Bengali fashion, was a great writer and a magnificent intellect, a highly civilized and elegant prosodist unfairly excoriated by Indians who had not read what they criticized. Some obituarists delighted in quoting the old curmudgeon's notorious dedication in *The Autobiography of an Unknown Indian:* "To the memory of the British Empire in India, which conferred subjecthood on us but withheld citizenship; to which yet every one of us threw out the challenge: *Civis Brittanicus Sum,* because all that was good and living within us was made, shaped and quickened by the same British rule." Most went on to say that outraged Indians did not read much more than the dedication; others pointed out, with a somewhat superior air, that the dedication was not the uncritical piece of British flattery it appeared to be, since, after all, it upbraided the Raj for denying British citizenship to Indians. Both sets of writers appeared to think that Indians who objected to Nirad-babu's autobiography were merely hypersensitive nationalists without the intelligence or discernment to know any better.

I beg to differ. However generously one reads that appalling dedication, there is no escaping the unedifying spectacle of a brown man with his nose up the colonial fundament. "All that was good and living within us" — all, mind you, not some — "was made, shaped and quickened" by British rule? The mind boggles at the thought of Nirad Chaudhuri's omissions, both of the millennial Indian civilizational and intellectual heritage, and of the exactions and injustices of British colonial rule. Any author who can put such a thought into the dedication of his first book is not merely being polemical; he is advertising his allegiances, and deserves to be taken at his own xenolatrous word.

Chaudhuri was the first Indian writer of any distinction to tap into the vein of an Indian national weakness — Indians' readiness, as a people, to lap up critical judgments about ourselves, especially if they have first been published abroad. I remember, as a child in the late 1960s, my mounting horror and indignation at reading an article by Niradbabu in the *Illustrated Weekly of India* entitled "Why I Hate Indians." Sure enough, it elicited a flurry of rejoinders that the editor, the puckish Khushwant Singh, published under the heading "Why I Hate Nirad Chaudhuri." But even then I wondered why the arrogant pedantry of the man, his sweeping generalizations and apocalyptic conclusions, usually unsupported by any empirical evidence, were taken so seriously by readers and editors.

Of course Nirad Chaudhuri was a man of learning and refinement. Of course he could quote Greek and Latin and drop classical allusions in a manner that went out of style with the solar topee. Of course he could write with elegance and erudition — though all too often his orotund sentences were weighed down by the turgidity of his vocabulary. Of course he was a literary original, in a way that was uniquely his own. But after granting all that, it is also true that he was a crotchety eccentric whose delight in his own iconoclasm showed little respect for the qualities and attainments of others. Nirad-babu was an Indian whose greatest satisfaction in his prospective bride lay in her ability to spell "Beethoven"; an Indian who thought more highly of Winston Churchill than he did of Mahatma Gandhi or Pandit Nehru. It was typical that his take-no-prisoners assault on all the citadels of Indian culture and civilization was titled *The Continent of Circe:* he had to turn to Western mythology even for his principal metaphor. *Civis Brittanicus Sum* indeed: no doubt woggishness loses something in the translation.

There is a great deal of truth in the indulgent suggestion by the American historian David Lelyveld that "Nirad Chaudhuri is a fiction created by the Indian writer of the same name — a bizarre, outrageous and magical transformation of that stock character of imperialist literature, the Bengali babu." The problem is that the caricatured babu was not transformed enough. While the British laughed at the breed for their half-successful attempts to emulate their English masters, Nirad-babu sought to demonstrate that his success was impossible to laugh at. In 1835, that archimperialist Lord Macaulay had envisaged the creation of an intermediate class of Indians, educated in English, to serve and support British rule: they would be "a class of persons Indian in blood and color but English in opinions, in morals, and in intellect." Not only did Nirad Chaudhuri teach himself to become the perfect English gentleman in terms of his intellect, tastes, and pro-imperial opinions (carrying the Macaulayan fantasy to its absurd extreme), but he went one better than most Englishmen, scattering phrases in French, German, and Italian through his writing.

Nirad-babu moved to England for good in 1970, but in his mind he had always lived there. Yet his writing itself evoked the Bengali babu's obsession with his lofty heritage, and his petulance at the failure of the white man to recognize and reward it. That there might be something faintly comical about the sight of this wizened figure, in his immaculate Bengali dhoti, strutting about Oxford lamenting the decline of British civilization does not seem to have occurred to his admirers. But then comedy is not what one thinks about at the crematorium.

# 14

# R. K. Narayan's Comedies of Suffering

WHEN THE NEWS BROKE IN 2001 of the ending of India's most distinguished literary career of the twentieth century, that of Rasipuram Krishnaswamy Narayanaswami (contracted, at Graham Greene's suggestion, to R. K. Narayan), who had passed away at ninety-two, I immediately received a number of calls from journalists and editors, mainly in the United States, who were hastily penning appreciations of the veteran writer. In every case, they asked for a contribution, a few lines, or at least a quote; in every case, I demurred. Death is a moment for regret, for retrospection and remembered affection, but I had little admiration to offer. At the same time, only once had I allowed the news of a writer's death to prompt me to pour vitriol onto his pyre, and that was when the Indophobic Nirad Chaudhuri went to his Elysian fields. I certainly did not feel so negatively about Narayan. Better to say nothing, I decided, when you have nothing much to say.

But the queries continued to come in, and once a

decent interval had passed, I agreed that perhaps the time had come to unburden myself. First of all, of a past wrong. Back in 1994, in a review of his *Grandmother's Tale* in the *New York Times*, I had criticized R. K. Narayan's writing in a manner that, I later learned, deeply hurt the old man. (I had not intended to, but was guilty, like most reviewers, of forgetting that writers, however eminent they may be, also have feelings.) My review also offended a number of friends I liked and respected — friends who accused me of lèse-majesté, iconoclasm, and Stephanian elitism, among other sins. So I suppose I had better explain myself.

To begin with, let me stress that my favorite Narayan story is the story of how he got his start as a novelist. "Some time in the early thirties," Graham Greene recalled, "an Indian friend of mine called Purna brought me a rather traveled and weary typescript — a novel written by a friend of his — and I let it lie on my desk for weeks unread until one rainy day. . . ." The English weather saved an Indian muse: Greene didn't know that the novel "had been rejected by half-a-dozen publishers and that Purna had been told by the author . . . to weight it with a stone and drop it into the Thames." Greene loved the novel, *Swami and Friends*, found a publisher for it in London, and so launched a career that was to encompass twenty-seven more books, including fourteen novels.

In giving him the Yatra Award for outstanding lifetime achievement — one of those Indian prizes that seem quite unable to sustain themselves, so that subsequent winners (if any) remain entirely unknown — the distinguished jury's citation declared Narayan "a master story-teller whose language is simple and unpretentious, whose wit is critical yet healing, whose characters are drawn with sharp precision and subtle irony, and whose narratives have the lightness of touch which only a craftsman of the highest order can risk." In the West, Narayan is widely considered the quintessential "Indian" writer, whose fiction evokes a sensibility and a rhythm older and less familiar to westerners than that of any other writer in the English language. My friends in India saw in Narayan our country's best hope of a Nobel Prize in Literature.

At his best, Narayan was a consummate teller of time-less tales, a meticulous recorder of the ironies of human life, an acute observer of the possibilities of the ordinary: India's answer to Jane Austen. The gentle wit, the simple sentences, the easy assumption of the inevitabilities of the tolerant Hindu social and philosophical system, the characteristically straightforward plotting, were all hallmarks of Narayan's charm and helped make many of his novels and stories in-teresting and often pleasurable.

But I felt that they also pointed to the banality of Narayan's concerns, the narrowness of his vision, the pre-dictability of his prose, and the shallowness of the pool of experience and vocabulary from which he drew. Like that of Austen, his fiction was restricted to the concerns of a small society portrayed with precision and empathy; unlike that of Austen, his prose could not elevate those concerns be-yond the ordinariness of its subjects. Narayan wrote of, and from, the mindset of the small-town South Indian Brahmin, and did not seem capable of a greater range. His metronomic style was frequently not equal to the demands of his situa-tions. Intense and potentially charged scenes were rendered bathetic by the inadequacy of the language used to describe them. In much of his writing, stories with extraordinary possibilities unfolded in flat, monotonous sentences that frustrated rather than convinced me, and in a tone that ranged from the clichéd to the flippant. At its worst, Narayan's prose was like the bullock-cart: a vehicle that can move only in one gear, is unable to turn, accelerate, or reverse, and remains yoked to traditional creatures who have long since been overtaken but know no better.

I was, I must admit, particularly frustrated to find that Narayan was indifferent to the wider canon of English fiction and to the use of the English language by other writers, Western or Indian. Worse, his indifference was something of which he was inordinately proud. He told interviewers that he avoided reading: "I don't admit influences." This showed in his writing, but he was defiant: "What is style?" he asked one interviewer. "Please ask these critics to first define it. . . . Style is a fad." The result was that he used words as if unconscious of their nuances: every other sentence included a word inappropriately or wrongly used; the ABC's of bad writing — archaisms, banalities, and clichés — abounded. It was as if the author had learned the words in a school textbook and imagined them hallowed by repetition rather than hollowed by regurgitation. Narayan's words were just what they seemed; there was no hint of meanings lurking behind the surface syllables, no shadow of worlds beyond the words. When asked why he didn't write in an Indian language, Narayan replied that he did, for English was an Indian language. Ironically, though, much of Narayan's prose reads like a translation.

Some of my friends felt I was wrong to focus on language — a writerly concern, as they saw it — and lose sight of the stories, which in many ways had an appeal that transcended language. But my point was that such pedestrian writing diminished Narayan's stories, undermined the characters, trivialized their concerns. Other serious readers of Narayan disagree with me, and perhaps so many of them can't be wrong. I was perhaps particularly unfair in suggesting that Narayan was merely a chronicler of the ordinary who reflected faithfully the worldview of a self-obsessed and complacent upper caste (and middle class). "I write primarily for myself," Narayan had said. "And I write about what interests me, human beings and human relationships. . . . Only the story matters; that's all." Fair enough: one should not expect Austen to be Orwell. But one does expect an Austen to enrich the possibilities of the language she uses, to illuminate her tools as well as her craft. Narayan's was an impoverished English, limited and conventional, its potential unexplored, its bones bare.

And yet my case was probably overstated. For there is enchantment in Narayan's world; his tales often captivate, even if they could have been better written. The world that emerges from his stories is one in which the family — or the lack of one — looms as the defining presence in each character's life; in which the ordinary individual comes to terms with the expectations of society; and in which these interactions afford opportunities for wry humor or understated pathos. Because of this, and because of their simplicity, the stories have a universal appeal, and are almost always absorbing. And they are infused with a Hindu humanism that is ultimately Narayan's most valuable characteristic, making even his most poignant stories comedies of suffering rather than tragedies of laughter.

So I, too, lament the great man's passing. "The only way to exist in harmony with Annamalai," Narayan wrote in one of his stories of a troublesome servant, "was to take him as he was; to improve or enlighten him would only exhaust the reformer and disrupt nature's design." Even the most grudging critic should not deny R. K. Narayan this self-created epitaph.

# 15

# The Enigma of Being V. S. Naipaul

F OR DECADES, THE POTTED BIOGRAPHY of V. S. Naipaul that
accompanies each of his more than twenty books has
carried the curious sentence, "After four years at Oxford he
began to write, and since then has followed no other profession." It is a fiercely idiosyncratic formulation, as if Naipaul
has defined his commitment to his craft by his unwilling-
ness to pursue any other. And it has stayed in my mind ever
since, in my teens, I first read Naipaul, as the biographical
hallmark of the True Writer, something that those of us who
labor at other employment can never really hope to be.

And yet it is only with the publication of the remarkable and moving collection of letters sent to and from the
adolescent "Vido" at Oxford (*Between Father and Son: Family
Letters*, edited by Naipaul's literary agent Gillon Aitken) that
I have fully understood the depth of meaning embodied in
that sentence. These letters, for the most part between
Naipaul and his father (even though many are addressed,
with undergraduate casualness, to "Dear Everybody"),

101

profoundly reflect both men's efforts to write successfully —
which is to say, to write well enough to be published or
broadcast, and above all, to be paid for it. They are full of
the pathos and struggle of writing — the creative blocks,
the malfunctioning typewriters, the distractions of work and
family, the depression-inducing rejections, and the anxious
accounting of remuneration for each completed effort — as
well as mutual appreciation, advice, and encouragement for
each other's work.

Naipaul *père* (referred to throughout as "Pa") was a
journalist and subeditor for the *Trinidad Guardian*, but really
wanted to write fiction. In his letters, Pa is burned up by the
struggle to make ends meet to support his growing family (a
seventh child is born in the course of this correspondence),
and burning, too, with envy of lesser writers who have at-
tained publication. His son, supplementing a government
scholarship at Oxford by living off funds he knows his father
can ill afford to send him, writes to pull himself out of the
dead-end middle-class penury to which a job in Trinidad
would have condemned him, as it condemned his father.
When Pa dies following a heart attack at the age of forty-
seven, it seems Vido will have to seek a job to support the
family. But a variety of international employment possibilities identified by the Oxford Appointments Committee —
from the United Nations to the Western India Match Company — fail to materialize. The choice is stark: return to
Trinidad (as one surmises his family would have wished) or
risk further poverty and failure by pursuing his literary am-
bitions (as his father would no doubt have wanted).

Naipaul persists, writing three books in a year. When,

toward the end of the collected correspondence, his first novel — *The Mystic Masseur* — is accepted for publication, we share the author's exhilaration, and celebrate the vindication it carries, not just of himself, but of his father. Comic and keenly observed, it is the kind of novel his father might have written — in a style that Naipaul himself would soon outgrow.

There is much material in the correspondence for the serious student of Naipaul's work, so much of which reflects the angularities of his personality. We read of his inability to accept "the responsibility of deserving affection" and of the nervous breakdown he attributes to "loneliness, and lack of affection." We learn repeatedly of his contempt for Trinidad, his dismissiveness toward acquaintances and relatives who do not measure up to his civilizational standards (all too often based on their failure to master the English language), and his awareness of his impact on others ("A friend told me the other day that people don't like me because I made them feel that I knew they were fools"). But we juxtapose these with the wise, compassionate, and invariably sound advice his father gives him in letter after letter on both life and literature. When Vido underlines his observation that "I think a man is doing his reporting well only when people start to hate him," his father replies, "I think it's the other way: a [writer] is doing his work well when people begin liking him." What a difference of worldviews lies between those lines! "Write sympathetically," Pa goes on — an injunction one wishes his increasingly acerbic and judgmental son had taken more to heart in the course of his distinguished but often dyspeptic writing career.

Writing sympathetically is not something V. S. Naipaul has done much of in his twenty-five books, which reveal many of the personal qualities that have made him so impressive, so readable, and yet so contrarian a writer. His novels are, to me, much the lesser achievement; his nonfiction, wrongheaded though it often is, is monumental. Naipaul's books of "journeys" and "excursions" are not quite travel books, though they are invariably about his own travels; they are not works of political scholarship, though they abound in political judgments; they are as much about himself — his ideas, values, prejudices, his own sense of dislocation as an Indian born in "unhallowed" Trinidad and settled in England — as they are about the countries he visits.

And yet sympathy has not been entirely lacking. Naipaul describes his method as that of a "discoverer of people, a finder-out of stories." In his books (most notably the curiously lumpy *India: A Million Mutinies Now*) he has tended to repeat verbatim long conversations with his interlocutors (not always getting them right, as some howlers in the *India* book testify), letting the stories go on when the reader is clamoring for interruption, context, analysis. But in his more recent works Naipaul injects himself a little more into the tales of the people he listens to, and even sometimes interprets them for the reader. His second book on Islam, *Beyond Belief*, is — despite the harshness of some of his depictions of Muslims — a more compassionate work than Naipaul's earlier books; whereas much of his nonfiction could be faulted for generalizing carelessly from small particulars, here Naipaul writes of individual needs, fears, and motivations with great delicacy and precision, and his individual cases have depth and humanity, while combining to make a compelling larger picture. Naipaul says the individual stories themselves are the point of his book: "the reader should not look for 'conclusions.'"

Naipaul's own sense of displacement, so effectively chronicled in his earlier books, most notably *The Enigma of Arrival*, is at the heart of his view of the world: his scathing contempt for "half-formed civilizations," his rejection of the passionate certitudes of those who act out a "rage" against a world that has advanced beyond their comprehension. In his books, he often spurns the "incompleteness" and "emptiness" of his native Trinidad, and dismisses people "without an idea of the future." This is a recurrent theme: in *Among the Believers* he poured contempt on Islam's failure to keep up with "the spread of universal civilization," arguing that "it was the late twentieth century — and not the faith — that could supply the answers." If he has begun to seem slightly less dismissive in his later work, some of his judgments of the Muslim world are no different from those he has levied at non-Islamic societies he has found similarly "half-formed," from India to Zaire.

Which is what makes those adolescent letters such curiously compelling reading. It is not just that we have seen what became of the young man with the fierce literary passion bubbling through the letters; it is that the letters themselves tell a story that almost exonerates the man the correspondent became. Reading the exchange between the youthful Naipaul and his father, one is enthralled as by a compelling epistolary novel, made all the more poignant by our foreknowledge of the tragedy that is to come (his father's premature and no doubt preventable death). And I, for one, caught up intensely in the family dramas detailed in these letters, could not help empathizing (as an Indian, as a writer, and as one-half of a very similar correspondence in my own college days) with many of the paternal and fraternal concerns they reflect. The fact that the famously curmudgeonly V. S. Naipaul kept these letters safe for the four decades that have passed since they were written tells us there is more to like about him than his books have ever revealed.

"I had always looked upon my life as a continuation of his," Naipaul wrote to his mother upon Pa's death, "a continuation which, I hoped, would also be a fulfillment." This it most emphatically is; and the reader cannot help sharing the Naipauls' heartbreak that his father did not live to savor his son's success. "I have no doubt whatever," Pa wrote to the eighteen-year-old Vido, "that you will be a great writer." He would have been proud beyond words that his Vido, now Sir Vidia Naipaul, "followed no other profession."

# 16

# Salman Rushdie: The Ground beneath His Feet

SIXTEEN VALENTINE'S DAYS AGO, Iran's Ayatollah Khomeini pronounced a fatwa, an Islamic edict, calling for the death of Salman Rushdie — and made the Indian-born British author of *The Satanic Verses* the most famous writer in the world. Yet the extent to which this controversy has dominated our perception of his work is itself an injustice. Mention Rushdie, and some see a stirring symbol of the cause of freedom of expression in the face of intolerant dogma; others, particularly in the Islamic world, find a blasphemous crusader for secularist social subversion. Neither image may be inaccurate, but reducing him to this emblematic figure has only served to obscure his true literary contribution — as, quite simply, one of the best and most important novelists of our time. As an Indian novelist, I can only repeat what Waugh said of Wodehouse: he is the head of my profession.

For Salman Rushdie has brought an astonishing new voice into the world of English-language fiction, a voice whose language and concerns stretched the boundaries of the possible in English literature. His heritage is derived from the polyglot tumult of multiethnic, postcolonial India; his intellectual convictions owe as much to Nehruvian nationalism and the eclecticism of the Sufi mystics as to any source west of the Suez; his style combines a formal English education with the cadences of the Indian oral storytelling tradition, the riches of Latin American magic realism, and the extravagant fabulism of the *Arabian Nights*. Both in his life and in his writing, Rushdie has stood for intermingling and interchange, displacement and transfiguration, migration and renewal. He recalled and reinvented his roots while thriving in his own uprootedness. With *Midnight's Children* he brought a larger world — a teeming, myth-infused, gaudy, exuberant, many-hued, and restless world — past the immigration inspectors of English literature. And he has enriched this new homeland with breathtaking, risk-ridden, imaginative prose of rare brilliance and originality.

In eight novels (of which I have only skipped the first, the reputedly impenetrable *Grimus*) Rushdie has developed his characteristic concerns with the great issues of our time. Themes of migration, innovation, conversion, separation, and transformation suffuse his work: exploration and discovery, faith and doubt, pluralism and purity, yearning and desire, infuse his fiction. And with all of Rushdie's novels, his story is also about the telling of stories. Above all, it would seem, of Indian stories, for Indian history, society, and contemporary politics are a rich lode he has profitably mined in all his books. India is, as ever, the intersection of the many strands of Rushdie's intellectual heritage, the womb of his imagination.

India — "that country without a middle register, that

continuum entirely composed of extremes" — is itself a character in many of his books. The author's farewell to it in *The Ground beneath Her Feet* is unbearably poignant: "India, my terra infirma. . . . India, my too-muchness, my everything at once, my mother, my father and my first great truth. . . . India, fount of my imagination, source of my savagery, breaker of my heart. Goodbye." But with Rushdie India always leads to the world; it is a mini-universe for a writer whose concerns are universal. "To provide for the planet's soul, there is India. One goes there as one goes to the bank, to refill the pocketbook of the psyche."

But what does the novelist fill it with? In a sadly overlooked passage of *The Satanic Verses*, Salman Rushdie writes of "the eclectic, hybridized nature of the Indian artistic tradition." Under the Mughals, he says, artists of different faiths and traditions were brought from many parts of India to work on a painting. One hand would paint the mosaic floors, another the human figures, a third the cloudy skies: "individual identity was submerged to create a many-headed, many-brushed 'Overartist' who, literally, was Indian painting." This evocative image could as well be applied to the nature of Indianness itself, the product of the same hybrid culture. How, after all, can one summarize the idea of the Indian identity? Any truism about India can be immediately contradicted by another truism about India. The country's national motto, emblazoned on its governmental crest, is "Satyameva Jayaté": Truth Alone Triumphs. The question remains, however: Whose truth? It is a question to which there are at least a billion answers — if the last census hasn't undercounted us again.

I raise the question of truth because, in the recent political campaigns in northern India, Prime Minister Atal Bihari Vajpayee apparently described the Congress Party leader, Sonia Gandhi, as a foreigner. When protests erupted, the PM said he was not casting aspersions on the leader of the opposition, merely stating a fact. But is it a fact? The renewed debate on the issue of Sonia Gandhi's eligibility to lead the country has brought to the forefront a vital question that has, in different ways, often engaged me — the question, Who is an Indian?

The last time this issue grabbed the headlines was nearly six years ago, when a crisis erupted in the Congress Party over the claim by three powerful Congress politicians, Sharad Pawar, Purno Sangma, and Tariq Anwar — with classic Congress secularism, a Hindu, a Christian, and a Muslim — that Mrs. Gandhi is unfit to be prime minister because she was born in Italy. In the extraordinary letter they delivered to her and leaked to the newspapers, the three party leaders declared, "It is not possible that a country of 980 million, with a wealth of education, competence and ability, can have anyone other than an Indian, born of Indian soil, to head its government." They went so far as to ask her to propose a constitutional amendment requiring that the offices of president and prime minister be held only by natural-born Indian citizens.

Of course there has been no such amendment, and the three Congress leaders are now ex-Congress leaders, having founded the Nationalist Congress Party instead to add to the splendid alphabet soup of political parties in our country. But their territorial notion of Indian nationhood is a curious one on many counts, and particularly so coming from long-standing members of the Indian National Congress, a party that was founded under a Scottish-born president, Allan Octavian Hume, in 1885 and among whose most redoubtable leaders (and elected presidents) was Annie Besant, who was born English, and Maulana Abul Kalam Azad, who was born in Mecca. Even more curious is the implicit repudiation of the views of the Congress's greatest-ever leader, Mahatma Gandhi, who tried to make the party a representative microcosm of an India he saw as eclectic, agglomerative, and diverse.

The three musketeers of the nativist revolt did, of course, anticipate this latter criticism. So they went out of their way to reinvent the Mahatma on their side. "India has always lived in the spirit of the Mahatma's words, 'Let the winds from all over sweep into my room,' " they wrote with fealty if not accuracy. "But again he said, 'I will not be swept off my feet.' We accept with interest and humility the best which we can gather from the north, south, east or west and we absorb them into our soil. But our inspiration, our soul, our honor, our pride, our dignity, is rooted in our soil. It has to be of this earth." The contradiction between their paraphrase of the Mahatma's views (absorbing the best from all directions) and their emotive "rooting" of "honor, pride and dignity" in the "soil" of "this earth" is so blatant it hardly needs pointing out. Yet it suffers a further inaccuracy: by law, even a "natural-born Indian" is one who has just one grandparent born in undivided India, as defined by the Government of India Act, 1935. You do not have to be of this soil to be an Indian by birth.

But Sonia Gandhi is, of course, an Indian by marriage and naturalization, not birth. So the usual chauvinists and xenophobes — not to mention the political opportunists of other stripes — have been quick to jump on the bandwagon started by the soil-sprung triumvirate. But is her western-ness immutably irreconcilable with their Indianness? In *The Ground beneath Her Feet* Rushdie brilliantly translates "disorientation" as "loss of the East." "Ask any navigator: the east is what you sail by. Lose the east and you lose your bearings, your certainties, your knowledge of what is and what may be, perhaps even your life." But not for Rushdie the flawed simplicity of the conventional encounters between East and West. The West, he points out, "was in Bombay from the beginning," in a land "where West, East, North and South had always been scrambled like codes, like eggs, and so Westernness was a legitimate part of Ormus, a Bombay part, inseparable from the rest of him."

So the truth may lie in a simple insight: as I have written in my book *India: From Midnight to the Millennium*, the singular thing about India is that you can only speak of it in the plural. There are, in the hackneyed phrase, many Indias. Everything exists in countless variants. If Americans can cite the national motto, "E Pluribus Unum," Indians can say, "E Pluribus Pluribum." There is no single standard, no fixed stereotype, no "one way." This pluralism is acknowledged in the way India arranges its own affairs: all groups, faiths, tastes, and ideologies survive and contend for their place in the sun. At a time when most developing countries opted for authoritarian models of government to promote nation-building and to direct development, India chose to be a multiparty democracy. And despite many stresses and strains, including twenty-two months of autocratic rule during a "state of emergency" declared by Prime Minister Indira Gandhi in 1975, a multiparty democracy — freewheeling, rumbustious, corrupt, and inefficient, perhaps, but nonetheless flourishing — India has remained.

One result is that India strikes many as maddening, chaotic, inefficient, and seemingly unpurposeful as it muddles through into the twenty-first century. Another, though, is that India is not just a country, it is an adventure, one in which all avenues are open and everything is possible. "India," wrote the British historian E. P. Thompson, "is perhaps the most important country for the future of the world. All the convergent influences of the world run through this society. . . . There is not a thought that is being thought in the West or East that is not active in some Indian mind."

That Indian mind has been shaped by remarkably diverse forces: ancient Hindu tradition, myth, and scripture; the impact of Islam and Christianity; and two centuries of British colonial rule. The result is unique. Many observers have been astonished by India's survival as a pluralist state. But India could hardly have survived as anything else. Pluralism is a reality that emerges from the very nature of the country; it is a choice made inevitable by India's geography and reaffirmed by its history.

One of the few generalizations that can safely be made about India is that nothing can be taken for granted about the country. Not even its name: for the word *India* comes from the river Indus, which flows in Pakistan. That anomaly is easily explained, for what is today Pakistan was part of India until the country was partitioned by the departing British in 1947. (Yet each explanation breeds another anomaly. Pakistan was created as a homeland for India's Muslims, but till very recently there were more Muslims in India than in Pakistan.)

With diversity emerging from its geography and inscribed in its history, India was made for pluralist democracy. It is not surprising, then, that the political life of modern India has been rather like traditional Indian music: the broad basic rules are firmly set, but within them one is free to improvise, unshackled by a written score. The music of India is the collective anthem of a hybrid civilization.

Over fifty-four years ago, at midnight on August 15, 1947, as the flames of communal hatred blazed across the land, independent India was born as its first prime minister, Jawaharlal Nehru, proclaimed "a tryst with destiny — a moment which comes but rarely in history, when we pass from the old to the new, when an age ends and when the soul of a nation, long suppressed, finds utterance." With those words he launched India on a remarkable experiment in governance — remarkable because it was happening at all. "India," Winston Churchill once barked, "is merely a geographical expression. It is no more a single country than the Equator." Churchill was rarely right about India, but it is true that no other country in the world embraces the extraordinary mixture of ethnic groups, the profusion of mutually incomprehensible languages, the varieties of topography and climate, the diversity of religions and cultural practices, and the range of levels of economic development that India does.

And yet India is more than the sum of its contradictions. It is a country held together, in Nehru's words, "by strong but invisible threads. . . . She is a myth and an idea," he wrote (Nehru always feminized India), "a dream and a vision, and yet very real and present and pervasive."

It has been over fifty-five years since that midnight moment when the British Empire in India came to an end amid the traumatic carnage of Partition with Pakistan and the sectarian violence that accompanied it. Yet in these last five decades of independence many thoughtful observers have seen a country more conscious than ever of what divides it: religion, region, caste, language, ethnicity. What makes India, then, a nation?

Let me turn again to an Italian example. No, not that Italian example. Amid the popular ferment that made an Italian nation out of a mosaic of principalities and statelets, one Italian nationalist memorably wrote, "We have created Italy. Now all we need to do is to create Italians." Oddly enough, no Indian nationalist succumbed to the temptation to express the same thought — "We have created India; now all we need to do is to create Indians."

Such a sentiment would not, in any case, have occurred to Nehru, that preeminent voice of Indian nationalism, because he believed in the existence of India and Indians for millennia before he gave words to their longings; he would never have spoken of "creating" India or Indians, merely of being the agent for the reassertion of what had always existed but had been long suppressed. Nonetheless, the India that was born in 1947 was in a very real sense a new creation: a state that had made fellow citizens of the Ladakhi and the Laccadivian for the first time, that divided Punjabi from Punjabi for the first time, that asked the Keralite peasant to feel allegiance to a Kashmiri Pandit ruling in Delhi, also for the first time. Nehru would not have written of the challenge of "creating" Indians, but creating Indians was what, in fact, the nationalist movement did.

When India celebrated the forty-ninth anniversary of its independence from British rule nine years ago, its then prime minister, H. D. Deve Gowda, stood at the ramparts of Delhi's sixteenth-century Red Fort and delivered the traditional Independence Day address to the nation in Hindi, India's "national language." Eight other prime ministers had done exactly the same thing forty-eight times before him, but what was unusual this time was that Deve Gowda, a southerner from the state of Karnataka, spoke to the country in a language of which he did not know a word. Tradition and politics required a speech in Hindi, so he gave one — the words having been written out for him in his native Kannada script, in which they, of course, made no sense.

Such an episode is almost inconceivable elsewhere, but it represents the best of the oddities that help make India India. Only in India could a country be ruled by a man who does not understand its "national language"; only in India, for that matter, is there a "national language" that half the population does not understand; and only in India could this particular solution be found to enable the prime minister to address his people. One of Indian cinema's finest "playback singers," the Keralite K. J. Yesudas, sang his way to the top of the Hindi music charts with lyrics in that language written in the Malayalam script for him, but to see the same practice elevated to the prime ministerial address on Independence Day was a startling affirmation of Indian pluralism.

We are all minorities in India. A typical Indian stepping off a train, a Hindi-speaking Hindu male from the Gangetic plain state of Uttar Pradesh, might cherish the illusion that he represents the "majority community," to use an expression much favored by the less industrious of our journalists. But he does not. As a Hindu he belongs to the faith adhered to by some 82 percent of the population, but a majority of the country does not speak Hindi; a majority does not hail from Uttar Pradesh; and if he were visiting, say, Kerala, he would discover that a majority is not even male. Worse, our archetypal UP Hindu has only to mingle with the polyglot, polychrome crowds thronging any of India's major railway stations to realize how much of a minority he really is. Even his Hinduism is no guarantee of majorityhood, because his caste automatically places him in a minority as well: if he is a Brahmin, 90 percent of his fellow Indians are not; if he is a Yadav, 85 percent of Indians are not, and so on.

Or take language. The constitution of India recognizes eighteen today (mirrored in the various scripts on the currency notes), but in fact there are thirty-five Indian languages that are spoken by more than a million people — and these are languages, with their own scripts, grammatical structures, and cultural assumptions, not just dialects (if we were to count dialects within these languages, there are more than 22,000). Each of the native speakers of these languages is in a linguistic minority, for none enjoys majority status in India. Thanks in part to the popularity of Bombay's Hindi cinema, Hindi is understood, if not always well spoken, by nearly half the population of India, but it is in no sense the language of the majority; indeed, its locutions, gender rules, and script are unfamiliar to most Indians in the south or northeast.

Ethnicity further complicates the notion of a majority community. Most of the time, an Indian's name immediately reveals where he is from and what his mother tongue is; when we introduce ourselves, we are advertising our origins. Despite some intermarriage at the elite levels in the cities, Indians still largely remain endogamous, and a Bengali is easily distinguished from a Punjabi. The difference this reflects is often more apparent than the elements of commonality. A Karnataka Brahmin shares his Hindu faith with a Bihari Kurmi, but feels little identity with him in respect of appearance, dress, customs, tastes, language, or political objectives. At the same time a Tamil Hindu would feel that he has far more in common with a Tamil Christian or Muslim than with, say, a Haryanvi Jat with whom he formally shares a religion.

Why do I harp on these differences? Only to make the point that Indian nationalism is a rare animal indeed. It is not based on language (since we have at least eighteen or thirty-five, depending on whether you follow the constitution or the ethnolinguists). It is not based on geography (the "natural" geographical frontiers of India have been hacked by the partition of 1947). It is not based on ethnicity (the "Indian" accommodates a diversity of racial types in which many Indians have more in common with foreigners than with other Indians — Indian Punjabis and Bengalis, for instance, have more in common with Pakistanis and Bangladeshis, respectively, than they do with Poonawalas or Bangaloreans). And it is not based on religion (we are home to every faith known to mankind, and Hinduism — a faith without a national organization, with no established church or ecclesiastical hierarchy, no uniform beliefs or modes of worship — exemplifies as much our diversity as it does our common cultural heritage). Indian nationalism is the nationalism of an idea, the idea of an ever-ever land — emerging from an ancient civilization, united by a shared history, sustained by pluralist democracy.

This land imposes no narrow conformities on its citizens: you can be many things and one thing. You can be a good Muslim, a good Keralite, and a good Indian all at once. Our founding fathers wrote a constitution for a dream; we have given passports to our ideals. Where Freudians note the distinctions that arise out of "the narcissism of minor differences," in India we celebrate the commonality of major differences. To stand Michael Ignatieff's famous phrase on its head, we are a land of belonging rather than of blood.

So the idea of India, to use Amartya Sen's phrase, is of one land embracing many. It is the idea that a nation may endure differences of caste, creed, color, culture, cuisine, conviction, costume, and custom, and still rally around a democratic consensus. That consensus is around the simple principle that in a democracy you don't really need to agree — except on the ground rules of how you will disagree. The reason India has survived all the stresses and strains that have beset it for fifty years, and that led so many to predict its imminent disintegration, is that it maintained consensus on how to manage without consensus.

Of course, not all agree with this vision of India. There are those who wish it to become a Hindu Rashtra, a land of and for the Hindu majority; they have made gains in recent elections and in the politics of the street. Secularism is established in India's constitution, but they ask why India should not, like many other Third World countries, find refuge in the assertion of its own religious identity. Recent news stories have chronicled the rise in Indian politics of an intolerant and destructive "Hindutva" movement that assaults India's minorities, especially its Muslims, that destroyed a well-known mosque and conducted horrific attacks on Muslims in the state of Gujarat, where in the twenty-first century men have been slaughtered because of the mark on a forehead or the absence of a foreskin. The votaries of this movement argue that only Hindus can be true Indians; Muslims and Christians, in particular, are deemed insufficiently Indian because their *punyabhoomi,* their holy land, lies outside the soil of India.

It is curious and sad to see the "two-nation theory" advocated by the supporters of Partition in the 1940s coming back to life in secular India six decades later. My generation (and Rushdie's) grew up in an India where our sense of nationhood lay in the slogan, "Unity in Diversity." We were brought up to take pluralism for granted, and to reject the communalism that had partitioned the nation when the British left. In rejecting the case for Partition, Indian nationalism also rejected the very idea that religion should be a determinant of nationhood. We never fell into the insidious trap of agreeing that, since Partition had established a state for Muslims, what remained was a state for Hindus. To accept the idea of India, you had to spurn the logic that had divided the country.

120

Western dictionaries define *secularism* as the absence of religion, but Indian secularism means a profusion of religions, none of which is privileged by the state, whose institutions are open to participation by everybody. Secularism in India does not mean irreligiousness, which even avowedly atheist parties like the Communists or the DMK have found unpopular among their voters; indeed, in Calcutta's annual Durga Puja, the youth wings of the Communist parties compete with each other to put up the most lavish Puja *pandals* or pavilions to the goddess Durga. Rather, it means, in the Indian tradition, multireligiousness. In the Calcutta neighborhood where I lived during my high school years, the wail of the muezzin calling the Islamic faithful to prayer blended with the tinkling bells and chanted mantras at the Hindu Shiva temple nearby and the crackling loudspeakers outside the Sikh *gurudwara* reciting verses from the Granth Sahib. (And St. Paul's Cathedral was only minutes away.)

The irony is that India's secular coexistence was paradoxically made possible by the fact that the overwhelming majority of Indians are Hindus. It is odd to read today of "Hindu fundamentalism," because Hinduism is a religion without fundamentals: no organized church, no compulsory beliefs or rites of worship, no single sacred book. The name itself denotes something less, and more, than a set of theological beliefs. In many languages — French and Persian among them — the word for "Indian" is *Hindu*. Originally *Hindu* simply meant the people beyond the river Sindhu, or Indus. But the Indus is now in Islamic Pakistan; and to make matters worse, the word *Hindu* did not exist in any Indian language till its use by foreigners gave Indians a term for self-definition.

"Hinduism" is thus the name others applied to the indigenous religion of India (*Sanatan Dharma*). It embraces an eclectic range of doctrines and practices, from pantheism to agnosticism and from faith in reincarnation to belief in the caste system. But none of these constitutes an obligatory credo for a Hindu: there are none. We have no compulsory dogmas. Hinduism is a civilization, not a creed that can be reduced to commandments.

The sectarian misuse of Hinduism for minority-bashing is especially sad since Hinduism provides the basis for a shared sense of common culture within India that has little to do with religion. The inauguration of a public project, the laying of a foundation stone, or the launching of a ship usually start with the ritual smashing of a coconut, an auspicious practice in Hinduism but one that most Indians of other faiths cheerfully accept in much the same spirit as a teetotaler acknowledges the role of champagne in a Western celebration. Hindu festivals, from Holi (when friends and strangers of all faiths are sprayed with colored water in a Dionysian ritual) to Deepavali (the festival of lights, firecrackers, and social gambling) have already gone beyond their religious origins to unite Indians of all faiths as a shared experience.

Festivals, *melas, lilas,* all "Hindu" in origin, have become occasions for the mingling of ordinary Indians of all backgrounds; indeed, for generations now, Muslim artisans in the Hindu holy city of Varanasi have made the traditional masks for the annual Ram Lila (the dance-drama depicting the tale of the divine god-king Rama). Hindu myths like the Ramayana and the Mahabharata provide a common idiom to all Indians, and it was not surprising that when national television broadcast a fifty-two-episode serialization of the Mahabharata, the script was written by a Muslim, Dr. Rahi Masoom Raza. Both Hindus and Muslims throng the tombs and *dargahs* of Sufi Muslim saints. Hindu devotional songs are magnificently sung by the Muslim Dagar brothers; the Hindu Shankar Shambhu invokes Muslim *pirs* as he chants the *qawwali*. Hinduism and Islam are intertwined in Indian life. In the Indian context today, it is possible to say that there is no Hinduism without Islam: the saffron and the green both belong on the Indian flag.

A lovely story that illustrates the cultural synthesis of Hinduism and Islam in India was recounted by two American scholars, Lloyd and Susan Rudolph. It seems an Indian Muslim girl was asked to participate in a small community drama about the life of Lord Krishna, the Hindu god adored by shepherdesses, who dance for his pleasure (and who exemplify through their passion the quest of the devout soul for the Lord). Her Muslim father forbade her to dance as a shepherdess with the other schoolgirls. In that case, said the drama's director, we will cast you as Krishna. All you have to do is stand there in the usual Krishna pose, a flute at your mouth. Her father consented; and so the Muslim girl played Krishna.

This is India's "secularism." Indeed, Hindus pride themselves on belonging to a religion of astonishing breadth and range of belief; a religion that acknowledges all ways of worshiping God as equally valid — indeed, the only major religion in the world that does not claim to be the only true religion. This eclectic and nondoctrinaire Hinduism — a faith without apostasy, where there are no heretics to cast out because there has never been any such thing as a Hindu heresy — is not the Hinduism professed by those who destroyed a mosque, nor the Hindutva spewed in hate-filled speeches by communal politicians. How can such a religion lend itself to "fundamentalism"? Hindu fundamentalism is a contradiction in terms, since Hinduism is a religion without fundamentals. India has survived the Aryans, the Mughals, the British; it has taken from each — language, art, food, learning — and grown with all of them. To be an Indian is to be part of an elusive dream all Indians share, a dream that fills our minds with sounds, words, flavors, from many sources that we cannot easily identify.

This is why the development of what has been called "Hindu fundamentalism" and the resultant change in the public discourse about Indianness is so dangerous. The suggestion that only a Hindu, and only a certain kind of Hindu, can be an authentic Indian is an affront to the very premise of Indian nationalism. The reduction of non-Hindus to second-class status in their homeland is unthinkable. It would be a second Partition: and a partition in the Indian soul would be as bad as a partition in the Indian soil. The only possible idea of India is that of a nation greater than the sum of its parts.

Of course it is true that, while Hinduism as a faith might privilege tolerance, this does not necessarily mean that all Hindus behave tolerantly. Ironically, Hindu chauvinism has emerged from the competition for resources in a contentious democracy. Politicians of all faiths across India seek to mobilize voters by appealing to narrow identities; by seeking votes in the name of religion, caste, and region, they have urged voters to define themselves on these lines. As religion, caste, and region have come to dominate public discourse, to some it has become more important to be a Muslim, a Bodo, or a Yadav than to be an Indian. But this is not merely dangerous; it is an assault on the essential underpinnings of Indianness.

Yet India's democracy helps to acknowledge and accommodate the various identities of its multifaceted population. No one identity can ever triumph in India: both the country's chronic pluralism and the logic of the electoral marketplace make this impossible. In leading a coalition government, the Hindu-inclined Bharatiya Janata Party has learned that any party ruling India has to reach out to other groups, other interests, other minorities. After all, there are too many diversities in our land for any one version of reality to be imposed on all of us.

So the Indian identity celebrates diversity: if America is a melting pot, then to me India is a *thali*, a selection of sumptuous dishes in different bowls. Each tastes different, and does not necessarily mix with the next, but they belong together on the same plate, and they complement each other in making the meal a satisfying repast. Indians are used to multiple identities and multiple loyalties, all coming together in allegiance to a larger idea of India, an India that safeguards the common space available to each identity. That is the tradition to which Rushdie's "Overartist" belonged.

At a time when the Huntington thesis of a "clash of civilizations" has gained currency, it is intriguing to contemplate a civilization predicated upon such diversity, one which provides the framework to absorb these clashes within itself. For Indians across the world, wary of the endless multiplication of sovereignties, hesitant before the clamor for division and self-assertion echoing in a hundred NRI forums, this may be something to think about. In today's globalized world, Indians in Michigan cannot escape identification with what is happening to Indians in Mumbai. So the idea of India is an idea familiar to Americans but few others — of a land where it doesn't matter what the color of your skin is, the kind of food you eat, the sounds you make when you speak, the God you choose to worship (or not), so long as you want to play by the same rules as everybody else, and dream the same dreams. If the overwhelming majority of a people share the political will for unity, if they wear the dust of a shared history on their foreheads and the mud of an uncertain future on their feet, and if they realize they are better off in Kozhikode or Kanpur dreaming the same dreams as those in Kohlapur or Kohima, a nation exists, celebrating diversity and freedom — and that is the India to which Rushdie's "Overartist" would belong.

To return, then, to Sonia Gandhi. Throughout its history the Congress Party has articulated and defended the idea that Indian nationalism is inclusive, tolerant, and pluralist, and that there are no acid tests of birth, religion, ethnicity, or even territory that disqualify one who wants to claim Indianness. As Ashutosh Varshney has pointed out, Sonia Gandhi "is an Indian — by her citizenship, by her act of living in India, and by the way she has adopted a new home. [A]n Indian is one who accepts the ethos of India."

Some, like the Samata Party spokeswoman, have claimed that Sonia "will never be able to fully understand the intricacies of our culture" because "cultural impulses are gained in the early stages of life." This argument is preposterous, since some of the greatest experts on Indian culture, who have forgotten more than most Indians will ever know about Bharatiya Sanskriti — from A. L. Basham to Richard Lannoy to R. C. Zaehner — are foreigners. Mani Shankar Aiyar turns the absurd "cultural" argument on its head by pointing out that "it is a disrespect to the millennial traditions of India to question the credentials of a daughter-in-law."

Sonia Gandhi herself has made her own case: "Though born in a foreign land, I chose India as my country," she points out. "I am Indian and shall remain so till my last breath. India is my motherland, dearer to me than my own life." But Sonia Gandhi is not the issue. The real issue is whether we should let politicians decide who is qualified to be an authentic Indian.

After the elections of 2004 Sonia Gandhi resolved the existential dilemma by winning election as the prime minister–designate of the ruling coalition and then renouncing the office in favor of another. The sight in May 2004 — in a country 82 percent Hindu — of a Roman Catholic leader (Sonia Gandhi) making way for a Sikh (Manmohan Singh) to be sworn in as prime minister by a Muslim (President Abdul Kalam) caught the world's imagination and won its admiration. No strutting nationalist chauvinism could ever have accomplished for India's standing in the world what that one moment did — all the more so since it was not directed at the world. It was an affirmation of an ancient civilizational ethos in a new political era, a moment that could have been torn from Rushdie's pages.

India has always proclaimed "unity in diversity," the idea of one land embracing many. You can be fair-skinned, sari-wearing, and Italian-speaking, and you are not more foreign to my grandmother in Kerala than someone who is "wheatish-complexioned," wears a *salwar-kameez*, and speaks Punjabi. Our nation absorbs both these types of people; both are equally "foreign" to some of us, equally Indian to us all. To start disqualifying Indian citizens from the privileges of Indianness is not just pernicious, it is an insult to the basic assumptions of Indian nationalism. An India that denies itself to some of us could end up being denied to all of us.

So who is an Indian? Anyone who wants to be, and is qualified by residence, allegiance, or citizenship. My India, like Salman Rushdie's, has room enough for everyone. In *The Moor's Last Sigh*, Moor (Moraes Zogoiby, the novel's narrator), celebrating his Catholic mother and Jewish father (and so referring to himself as a "cathjew nut"), has a metaphorical role as a symbol of Rushdie's India, a "unifier of opposites, a standard-bearer of pluralism" who in his mother's last paintings descends into "a semi-allegorical figure of decay." India is, as ever, not just a nation but a literary device, the intersection of the many strands of Rushdie's intellectual heritage — an eclectic palimpsest repeatedly painted over by history and myth, by colonial traders and settlers, by the English language, and by the tragic majesty of Islam, symbolized by the placing of the Alhambra on Bombay's Malabar Hill, the author's childhood address. The novel is suffused with nostalgia for an India much loved and, like King Boabdil's Granada, lost (at the time of its writing, it must have seemed irretrievably lost) to the exiled writer. The sultan in *The Moor's Last Sigh* weeps for the world he has given up, for the history he has betrayed, the tradition he has failed to defend; he sighs for a loss that is intensely personal and yet of far greater significance than his own person. In this novel Rushdie too, through his own moor, sighs upon his loss of the India he had known and loved and believed he might never be able to visit in safety again; but also for the greater loss of the secular, multireligious, pluriethnic India of which he has written with such passion and pride.

That India, though, still exists; it has not yet fallen to the bombs and the bigotry of the chauvinists and corrupt opportunists this novel excoriates. We need not spend much time on them; as Rushdie wrote of a Bombay building populated by the nouveau riche: "Everest Vilas is twenty-nine stories high, but mercifully these are stories I do not need to tell." The Indian idea — that people of every imaginable color, creed, caste, cuisine, and consonant can live and strive and triumph together in one gloriously mongrel nation — is more relevant than ever, and it has no abler advocate than Salman Rushdie. He has become, as much for his convictions as for his creativity, the finest English writer of India, and the most gifted reinventor of Indianness since Nehru. Perhaps, as Rushdie himself has written, "the only people who see the whole picture are the ones who step out of the frame."

The "permeation of the real world by the fictional is a

symptom of the moral decay of our post-millennial culture," declaims the anonymous narrator of one of the stories in Rushdie's collection *East, West.* "There can be little doubt that a large majority of us opposes the free, unrestricted migration of imaginary beings into an already damaged reality, whose resources diminish by the day." Rushdie's tongue is of course firmly in his cheek here, but it is the free, unrestricted migration of his imagination that can help heal the tragic damage done to the reality of Indianness — an Indianness that his writing so remarkably celebrates.

# III

## The Literary Life

# 17

# Rushdie's Reappearance

LITERARY FESTIVALS ARE RARELY NEWSWORTHY EVENTS; not real news, anyway. They are occasions for authors to get together, wallow in self-congratulation, and persuade themselves that they are performing a public service in the bargain. Writers come, confer, and consume, and literature serves only to provide a unifying purpose under the cover of which a good time is had by all. The emphasis is usually on conviviality, not controversy.

A rare exception occurred, however, at the Sunday Times Hay-on-Wye Festival of Literature in 1992. Britain's premier literary event is actually more pleasant than most, a cheerful occasion set in the picturesque surroundings of the Welsh countryside. Hay-on-Wye nestles among rolling hills, a town of 5,000 which boasts a ruined castle, one first-class hotel — and thirty-four bookshops. And it was here that news was made when Salman Rushdie first emerged from hiding.

I was there myself, to read from *The Great Indian Novel* and to participate in a panel discussion on Wodehouse and the English comic novel. On the afternoon in question the program announced a talk between Martin Amis, son of Kingsley (and reigning enfant terrible of British letters), and Israeli novelist David Grossman. The pairing was doubly intriguing, since Amis had attracted a great deal of criticism in Jewish circles for his last novel, *Time's Arrow*, a sort of deconstructionist view of the Holocaust whose narrative goes backward in time, like a film run the wrong way through the projector. The near-capacity crowd was thus looking forward to a literary exchange with sharp political overtones. They were to get one, but not quite in the way they expected.

On the morning of the event, word went round the festival that the place was "crawling with Special Branch detectives." Since Scotland Yard does not usually trouble itself with mere writers, speculation mounted. "I've heard the Israeli ambassador is coming," one local announced authoritatively. Having been tipped off the previous day, it was all I could do to hold my tongue.

At the appointed hour, Peter Florence, the young actor who runs the festival, stepped onto the stage. "I regret to announce," he said, "that David Grossman cannot be with us today." Murmurs of dismay filled the hall. "Martin Amis, however, is here. I wrote to him the other day to say that one could not imagine a British literary festival without him. The same is true, of course, of the author who is replacing David Grossman today — Salman Rushdie."

For one disbelieving moment there was an astonished silence. Rushdie had been in hiding for three years, with a price upon his head. Then, as Peter Florence's words sank in, a torrent of applause erupted. Rushdie and Amis walked onto the stage, clad — by bizarre coincidence — in identical khaki suits, intellectuals dressed for war. The audience gave them a standing ovation.

The conversation that followed was enthralling for Rushdie's fans, though those who had kept close track of the Rushdie affair over the three years since a fatwa had taken his freedom away from him had heard or read much along the same lines. But there were still three things Rushdie said that were news to much of the audience, including me. First, he mentioned that a pirated Farsi translation of *Shame* had won a literary prize in Iran the year before Ayatollah Khomeini's fatwa on *The Satanic Verses.* Second, Rushdie publicly recanted his Christmas 1990 reconversion to Islam in terms more explicit than I had heard before, saying it was his only regret, an insincere attempt to save his skin. Third, he moved away from the "I can't understand what the fuss is all about — this is only a novel" line that many Indians had seen as evidence of either disingenuousness or deracination. Instead, he admitted he had expected *The Satanic Verses* to provoke Muslims, to stimulate debate, even controversy; what he had not expected was the ultimate attempt to silence his apostasy, a sentence of death.

This was a more credible line of defense than he has used in the past. "Shashi Tharoor knows," he told his British audience, "that there are a couple of Muslim critics in India who'll attack me whatever I write. I expected that, and I expected to be able to respond to them, to engage in a public debate on their criticisms. I did not expect this."

Later, I asked Salman Rushdie whether the time had not come for Indians of his background — Indians, I dare say, like myself — to reclaim him for ourselves, to stop allowing him to be defined by his Western supporters. After all, he was preeminently the writer who had given voice to the sensibility of the secular urban subcontinental. What he stands for as the author of *Midnight's Children* alone should mean far more to us Indians than a couple of pages torn out of context from *The Satanic Verses*. How did he feel about the terms in which his supporters in the West have cast him — including as an excuse for bigoted attacks on Islam that, in happier times, he might have rejected? Had his feelings changed about his connection to the Indian constituency from which he had emerged?

Rushdie answered the second question with a moving evocation of how much India, and Bombay in particular, meant to him and how much it hurt that he could not walk its streets again without fear of being lynched. In the process, he deftly sidestepped the first question. I thought it ungracious to insist upon an answer. A man in his position is grateful for his defenders; he cannot afford to be choosy about the terms of their defense.

And so Salman Rushdie was whisked away by his police escort, a haunted symbol of Western literary freedom under assault from Oriental despotism, rather than the voice of the Muslim immigrant in the West that he had sought to be. Before he left, I shook his hand and wished him well. He thanked me for a letter of support I had sent him. I wanted to say I wished he would one day no longer need such support. But the words did not come. I hoped the day soon would.

# 18

# Books and Botox

A MERICANS, THE CONVENTIONAL WISDOM HAS IT, don't read. At least not as much as they used to. Television, movies, computer games, the Internet — all have driven people away from books. And when they do read, it seems it's not literature they want. The best-seller lists are overflowing with diet books, books on self-improvement, books on how to play the dating game. The fiction lists seem to consist of nothing but steamy romances and formulaic thrillers. "Americans," a British academic once growled to me, "don't know the difference between wanting to read a book and wanting a book to read."

So it was with decidedly mixed feelings that I found myself at what is billed as America's largest literary gathering, the *Los Angeles Times* Festival of Books, an annual event that overwhelms the University of California's UCLA campus on the last weekend in April. Could the home of Hollywood and Burbank, capital of the mass entertainment industry, better known for its trivial game shows and glittering but insubstantial soirées, truly celebrate something as solitary and unglamorous as reading?

Apparently 400 authors and 250 exhibitors thought so. So did an astonishing 125,000 people who thronged the festival over the weekend to hear authors ranging from Salman Rushdie to Sharon Roan, author of *Our Daughters' Health*. There were the usual readings and signings, including one tracing "The Evolution of a Book: From Inspiration to Publication." There were discussions on topics from "Is Geography Fate? Reflections on the East," featuring two British writers and your faithful correspondent, to "Do Books Have a Future?" (The answer was apparently a qualified yes.)

But this being L.A., the truly Big Moment was an awards ceremony: the year's *Los Angeles Times* Book Prizes, from poetry to fiction. Entering from Sunset Boulevard, I couldn't help thinking of that other L.A. awards ceremony — the Oscars. But the invitation prosaically required "business attire," and there wasn't a shimmering blond in sight. Instead of the collagen-enhanced, serenely Botoxed faces and figures that would be on hand to celebrate the silver screen, here we floated on a sea of wrinkles, furrowed brows, eyes narrowed from squinting at the page — or the computer monitor. Last year, author Frank McCourt had taken the mike to clamor for more cleavage at the event. It did not seem that he had got his way. Books and Botox, it seems, don't go together.

Hollywood casts a long shadow, however: the director of the Book Prize turned out to be a film critic. A giant fake bookcase dominated the stage, framing a high-resolution television screen featuring the photos and book covers of short-listed nominees. As the prizes were announced, there was the inevitable fumbling with the envelope as tension mounted — then the sweet high of triumph. Gasps and shrieks rose from the audience, or at least that portion loyal to the winner, none louder than those greeting the winner of "Best Mystery/Thriller." A spotlight plucked her from the applauding masses as she accepted embraces from family and friends, then strode briskly to the stage — our thrilled and mysterious laureate, a matronly figure in an unpretentious pantsuit.

If that showed the limits of the Oscar parallel, the acceptance speeches were all too familiar. Fervent gratitude to editors, publishers, and publicists is, alas, no more exciting to hear than teary lists of thanks to producers, directors, and publicists. All hail the biography prizewinner whose entire remarks consisted of the sentence, "I will not start thanking people because I couldn't stop." But then his book has a long list of acknowledgments.

The book fair brought home a fact I'd long known but never fully appreciated. Americans are great at making occasions out of next to nothing; in literature as in life, presentation is as important as substance, and there's nothing worthwhile that couldn't be improved by better packaging. The great American tautology is probably, "You can't succeed if you're not promoted." No writer is too eminent to need marketing, and no publicity is beneath a successful American writer. Serious novelists appear on the *Today* show to be quizzed about their lifestyles by interviewers who haven't cracked the covers of their books. The talk show hostess Oprah Winfrey can catapult an unknown into bestsellerdom with five minutes of breathless airtime. When the writer Jonathan Franzen was careless enough to express disdain for her taste, Oprah's decision to disinvite him became the major literary story of the month, eclipsing any headlines his actual appearance might have garnered.

Perhaps that's the only way literature will survive in America. Amid the general atmosphere of celebration at the awards ceremony, Steve Wasserman of the *Los Angeles Times*, editor of what is perhaps the country's most cerebral book section, sounded a grim warning. The next day the *San Francisco Chronicle* was to close its separate book review section, collapsing it into its entertainment section. The *Boston Globe*, despite appearing in a city famed for its fifty institutions of higher learning, was about to do the same. The *San Jose Mercury*, publishing in the heart of America's most prosperous area, Silicon Valley, had cut its book-review pages by a third. Even the venerable *New York Times* was to reduce the country's grandest and most widely read book review from thirty-six pages to thirty-two. And there was talk of making the *New York Times Book Review* more appealing to a general readership by requiring its editors to deign to notice popular fiction — the sort of books that regularly dominated the *Book Review*'s best-seller lists but rarely commanded review space in its columns.

Ironically, many publishers quietly welcomed the *San Francisco Chronicle*'s action. Entertainment sections of newspapers always have attracted more readers than book review sections, and advertisements for books would therefore reach a larger readership if they appeared under the entertainment rubric. It's an odd way to look at it, but I could see the point. It's a reminder that in America, literature, too, is a business. I noticed that the actress who provides the voice of Bart Simpson on the animated TV show *The Simpsons* was a major draw at the festival, helping sell a number of volumes based on the popular cartoon series. Those are the kinds of things that help sustain publishers' profits — and the reading habit. If there were a Best Supporting Author award, I'd have been glad to give it to her.

# 19

# Illiteracy in America

THE YOUNG BLACK MAN THRUST A PAPER AT ME, squinting into the sun. "Hey, man, can you tell me where this is?" he asked.

I was a visitor to Detroit myself, but one glance at the scribbled address told me the answer to his question. I pointed at the street sign barely fifteen feet away, which he couldn't possibly have missed. "It's right there," I said, adding with unnecessary cruelty: "Can't you see the street sign?"

He looked sheepishly at me, pulled the paper back, and shuffled toward the corner. And then it hit me. The reason he had had to ask me, a stranger standing on the sidewalk, was not because he hadn't seen the sign. It was because he couldn't read it.

He was not alone. An astonishing 47 percent of Detroiters, nearly one out of two adults in this predominantly black city, are functionally illiterate. (By way of comparison, the figure for Vietnam is 6.7 percent.) Functional illiteracy relates to the inability of an individual to use reading, writing, and computational skills in everyday life situations: filling out a job application, reading traffic signs, figuring out an election ballot, reading a newspaper, understanding a bus schedule or a product label — or an address on a sheet of paper. In the richest country on earth, 23 percent of adult Americans — forty-four million men and women — cannot do these things. Detroit is the worst case, but it's only twice as bad as the rest of the country.

The situation is in fact even worse than that suggests, because another 50 million Americans cannot read or comprehend above the eighth-grade level. To understand what that means: you need ninth-grade-level comprehension to understand the instructions for an antidote on an ordinary can of cockroach poison in your kitchen, tenth-grade level to follow a federal income tax return, twelfth-grade competence to read a life insurance form. Nearly half of America's adults cannot do these things. They are, in effect, unequipped for life in a modern society.

If it's startling enough for foreigners to realize there is such a thing as American illiteracy, what's poignant is that, unlike in the developing world, where illiteracy is predominantly a rural problem, in the United States it occurs overwhelmingly in the inner cities, with a heavy concentration among the poor and those dependent on welfare. I was in Detroit to address a conference on the crisis in America's cities, and I had stepped out onto the street to get some fresh air and use my cell phone while awaiting my turn to speak. In the young man in front of me I saw the problem there at its worst. Nearly half of Detroit's citizens between the ages of sixteen and sixty, I was told, are jobless and not seeking work. Why? It's a fair guess that most of them do not have the required literacy skills to apply for the available jobs, or even to be trained for them.

An outspoken civic worker I met told me that illiteracy and unemployment go hand-in-hand: 70 percent of functionally illiterate adults have no job or only a part-time job. Those who are employed have it tough. Illiterate adults work an average of nineteen weeks a year, compared to forty-four weeks a year for literates. Workers without a high school degree earn four times less than those with a college degree. And they often can't cope at work. Business losses attributable to literacy deficiencies in America cost the country tens of billions of dollars every year in low productivity, errors by workers who can't read properly, industrial accidents, lawsuits, and poor product quality.

What's worse, the standards and requirements for literacy have increased in recent years, as computerization has taken over the world. "You've got mail" may be the defining slogan of our age, but it excludes those who can't decipher their mail, electronic or otherwise. In a world where you can tell the rich from the poor by their Internet connections, the poverty line trips over the high-speed digital line. The key to the computer age is the keyboard, but too many Americans literally cannot read the keys. No wonder 70 percent of mothers on welfare have low literacy skills. Since they are unable to help their children to read or write, illiterate parents have children who struggle to read and drop out of school, perpetuating the problem down the generations. The cost in terms of the loss of human potential is devastating. But there's an impact on crime too: 60 percent of all juvenile offenders have illiteracy problems. Adults are no better — seven out of ten prisoners have low literacy levels, and the current prison population of two million represents a dramatic concentration of illiterate Americans. They know how to fire a gun but not how to read the Bible. Even the NRA couldn't be entirely happy with that.

It's worrying to realize how many Americans are handicapped in their ability to participate in this complex modern society. The young man at that Detroit street corner will always have to rely on others for vital information to lead his life; he will always be vulnerable to abuse and exploitation by those who can wield that one vital skill he doesn't have — the ability to make sense out of the shapes on a printed page, or on a street sign. And this in the world's oldest and most powerful democracy, whose citizenry make (or acquiesce in) decisions that affect the rest of the world.

I ran after the young man and caught up with him at the light. "Here, let me help," I said, taking the paper from him and reading the address aloud. "That should be that building over there," I said, pointing at a building half a block away, its name visible in large lettering above the entrance. He looked at me in gratitude, but I just felt helpless. I wished I had a leaflet on me for an adult remedial education program — but he wouldn't be able to read that either.

"Thanks, man," he said, a delighted look in his eyes. He headed off — this time, at least, in the right direction.

# 20

# The Great American Literary Illusion

H<small>AVE YOU HEARD?</small>" chortled my friend the literary agent. "Apparently, eighty-one percent of Americans feel they should write a book."

She wasn't kidding. Eighty-one percent of the citizenry of the land of the free and the home of the brave think they have a book in them. That's according to a survey of 1,006 adult Americans commissioned by the Jenkins Group, a Michigan publishing services firm. Having just established, in the course of researching the article preceding this one, that a staggering percentage of Americans are in fact functionally illiterate, I was astonished to discover the even more staggering percentage that saw themselves as pregnant with best-sellers just waiting to be born.

This should not in fact have surprised me, because I've met Carlos the doorman. Carlos presides, in green uniform and peaked cap, over the reception desk at one of New York City's tonier addresses, the kind where all visitors have to be announced but there is no sign crassly telling them so.

One day the friend I was visiting happened to mention to Carlos that I was an author. "Really?" he beamed, his smile equal parts admiration and complicity. "I'm by way of being an author myself." It turned out he'd been working sporadically on a tell-all, spare-no-one, bodice-ripping yarn about the inhabitants of a tony apartment building on the West Side. "When I'm sitting here, helping the residents with their problems, I'm not just no doorman," he confessed. "I'm doing me research."

Good luck to him, of course. And it's probably just what the market needs, so I thought better of giving him a quick primer on the libel laws. After all, this is the year that two New York nannies turned their thinly disguised experiences mentoring the mewling offspring of Park Avenue parents into the best-selling, soon-to-be-a-major-motion-picture book *The Nanny Diaries*. If two nannies can mine their months of child-minding to such runaway success, who's to say Carlos can't find gold amid the packages he signs for, the visitors he announces, and the food deliveries he sends up every day?

In fact Jenkins estimates that six million Americans have actually written a manuscript. The number sounds grim enough, but it's grimmer still when you realize that only some 80,000 books get published each year. So the manuscript-writing multitudes are being met by the implacable resistance of a tiny minority of publishers churning out rejection slips. No wonder there's a boom in independent publishing and self-publication, two practices that have helped increase the number of books annually making it into print. Ironically, book publishing may be the only growth industry left in the current economy.

But if Carlos has a lot of competition, as a budding novelist he's better off than most. Jenkins noted that only about a quarter of Americans say they would, given the opportunity, write a work of fiction. The overwhelming majority of prospective authors responding to the poll see themselves writing nonfiction. Most spoke, with commendable altruism and complete lack of imagination, of writing books that would help other people: inspirational self-help volumes, do-it-yourself guides, or that hardy perennial, cookbooks. Those are, of course, the categories that sustain most American best-seller lists.

What explains this general enthusiasm, not just for the printed word, but for actually producing it? America, the land of 113 cable TV channels and three telephones per inhabitant, hardly strikes the average foreign visitor as a haven for the Book. It may be counterintuitive, but one explanation could well lie in the computer revolution. Now people who can't spell have begun to write. The ether overflows with personal Web sites and weblogs, not to mention e-mails, whose number doubles every three months. It's not such a great leap from writing and sending an e-mail to developing a Web site or a "blog" and then persuading yourself that the next step is a book. After all, some e-mails have a larger readership than the average first novel.

Another reason, though, is as American as cheeseburger. It's the nature of American democracy, that great leveler. This is a country whose people really believe that anyone can be president; what's so different about the proposition that anyone can write a book? (Not to mention that it's a lot cheaper than running for president.) "I've read a lotta books, sittin' here," Carlos told me. "And I said to my-self, heck, I can do better'n that."

He may be right: there's an awful lot of awful books be-ing published these days, some of which end up on the best-seller lists. The question that is not asked by all these prospective authors is whether the book would be worth reading, whether it would add in some way to the sum total of humanity's cultural heritage. The only question they be-lieve they need to ask is that other great American question: Will it sell?

"How's the book going?" I asked Carlos the other day as I caught him at his desk in a reverie, tapping his chin with a pencil, a faraway look in his eyes. "Oh, not bad so far, Mr. T," he replied hastily. And then, as if to explain his abstrac-tion, he added: "I was just thinking about the sequel."

Maybe 81 percent is an undercount.

# 21

# Literature, *S'Il Vous Plait*

TRUST THE FRENCH. Who else would have put so much energy and resources into bringing twenty Indian writers to their country for a series of "rencontres" with the public of this highly literate land? At a time when readership for literary novels is dropping everywhere like the stock market index, France remains devoutly wedded to the promotion and propagation of culture. And not just its own. Every year the French equivalent of the Sahitya Akademi — the Centre National du Livre — picks one or two countries and brings a selection of its writers to the Continent for a two-week program known as the "Belles Etrangères." The year 2002 marked India's turn.

Nineteen of us — we should have been twenty, but one Marathi writer, Kishor Shantabai Kale, was held up by the courts after his father-in-law, another writer, brought a case against him — spent the second half of November waxing literary under the gray skies of a drizzly Continent. It was an impressively motley group. Five septuagenarian seniors — the legendary Mahasweta Devi, Jnanpith and Mag-saysay Award–winning Bengali novelist and social activist; the distinguished U. R. Ananthamurthy, Kannada novelist and former president of the Sahitya Akademi; the Rajya Sabha MP and Telugu poet C. Narayana Reddy; and the eminent Hindi stylists Nirmal Verma and Krishna Baldev Vaid — were joined by a variety of younger writers in other languages. We spanned the range from the trilingual sixty-year-old M. Mukundan, a product of the former French territory of Mahé in Kerala who has published dozens of books in Malayalam, to the U.S.-based thirty-one-year-old Akhil Sharma, who is working on his second novel. In between were the Dalit writers Bama (Tamil) and Narendra Jadhav (Marathi), the Hindi poet Udayan Vajpeyi, the Gujarati Jewish memoirist and novelist Esther David, the youngest-ever Jnanpith winner (for her Hindi novel *Kali-katha via Bypass*), Alka Saraogi, and five more English-language novelists (in alphabetical order), Anita Rau Badami, Shauna Singh Baldwin, Upamanyu Chatterjee, Mukul Kesavan, and myself. The list was completed by the author-illustrator pair of Anushka Ravishankar and Pulak Biswas, who found enthusiastic audiences of children throughout.

Some of us worried about the burden of being expected to "represent" Indian literature: there was nothing particularly democratic or incontestable about our selection and I, for one, lamented the absence of an Indian Muslim voice. (It turned out that Soraiya Bibi, the former Kamala Das, had dropped out at the last minute, the great Urdu novelist Qurratulain Hyder had been unable to travel, and a third Muslim invitee had been laid low by a stroke.) There

was also the question about what made us all "Indian": five
of the nineteen currently live abroad, and three (Badami,
Baldwin, and Sharma) who have permanently made their
homes elsewhere no longer carry Indian passports. Is Indianness, then, a state of mind, or a badge of ethnicity? Nine
Indian languages (including English) were represented; what
about the other nine that figure on our rupee notes? The im-
possibility of doing justice to the breadth of Indian writing
within a logistically manageable number of writers pointed
to the unfairness of the question. What we all had in common was that some of our work was available in French
translation, that the event's literary adviser, the Paris-based
Rajesh Sharma, had considered us worth inviting, and that we
were all able to get away when the French wanted us. In the
absence of other defensible criteria, that would have to do.

After a couple of joint events we scattered throughout
France in smaller groups, and some us were even asked to
make brief forays to Belgium and Holland. But the time we
spent together was among the highlights of the trip — the
opportunity for nineteen Indian writers to get to know each
other better, to convert names we had heard into flesh-and-
blood companions whose voices, tastes, and foibles added
an invaluable dimension to their literary reputations. The
literary encounters were fun, but nothing could match the
joy of being embraced by the gentle affection of Mahasweta
Devi, or making up for the inadequacies of French vegetar-
ian fare by dipping into the bottles of *chilli-achaar* (hot pep-
per pickle) that Alka Saragi had so thoughtfully brought
along. If in the process we could also encourage the French
public to read more about India — and embolden French

publishers to go on to discover other Indian authors — so much the better.

The writers left France at the beginning of December full of tales of their experiences: of being received by the dynamically articulate French foreign minister, Dominique de Villepin (a veteran of the French embassy in Delhi), whose discourse ranged from the importance of retaining a plurality of literary voices to the prospects of war over Iraq; of being startled when Narayana Reddy thereupon broke into a melodic Telugu chant, the likes of which had never been heard in the meeting rooms of the quai d'Orsay; of Bama being heckled by Tamil expatriates in Paris for drawing attention in France to the problems of untouchability, and of Esther David rising to her defense; of Shauna Singh Baldwin making side trips to assorted French cities where much of the action of her next novel is to take place; of an overflowing reception by the Indian ambassador, Savitri Kunadi, with writers, publishers, editors, and translators downing champagne and samosas; and for me, of having to juggle readings and responses in both English and French, as a packed audience at the city's Maison de l'Inde (House of India) included equal numbers of people who did not know one or the other of these languages.

But the defining moment of the trip came toward the end of the fortnight, when the group, returning from a reception at the majestic Hotel de Ville, found themselves accidental witnesses to the interment of the nineteenth-century novelist Alexandre Dumas, more than a century after his death, in the magnificently lit Pantheon. The Roman columns of this great Parisian monument were bathed in purple, red, and blue light; a military band played outside, while an honor guard escorted the coffin of the author of *The Three Musketeers* to its final resting place. Ananthamurthy, the doyen of the group, put it simply to me. "The French," he said, "really know how to honor their writers."

And — in a smaller way — ours too.

## 22

# Bharatiya Sanskriti in the Big Apple

QUIZ QUESTION FOR THE LITERARY-MINDED: where in the world did many of the giants of Indian literature gather at the end of September 2003 for an *Akhil Bharatiya Sahitya Sammelan* (All-India Literary Conference) inaugurated by Prime Minister Atal BihariVajpayee? New Delhi, the capital of India? Nope. Calcutta, the capital of everything cultural? *Nahin.* First prize for the smart kid in the back row who said "New York."

Yes, it was in the unlikely setting of New York, in a building uncompromisingly called the Manhattan Center, that you could hear, over three days, Gulzar declaim his Urdu poetry, Sunil Gangopadhyay speak about the Bengali novel, and M. T. Vasudevan Nair explain the history of Malayalam fiction, as the head of the Sahitya Akademi, Dr. Gopichand Narang, presided. This extraordinary event, which drew crowds ranging from a hundred to five hundred expatriates on each of the three days, was an initiative of the Bharatiya Vidya Bhavan, the unheralded institution devoted

155

to promoting Indian culture. And it proved a triumph for one man who, in the Big Apple, is synonymous with the institution — the indefatigable septuagenarian Dr. P. Jayaraman, a Madrasi who writes books in *shuddh* Hindi and who, in New York, *is* the Bhavan.

So New Yorkers were treated to an experience you would be hard-pressed to find in any of our major metropolises in India: a *kavi sammelan* (poetry slam) featuring the likes of Gulzar, the Marathi poet Dilip Chitre, the Kannada poets Chandrasekhar Kambar and Vaidehi, the Oriya poet Harprasad Das, the Urdu poets Bashir Badr and Shahryar; a panel discussion chaired by Nirmal Verma in which the Hindi novelist Kamleshwar rubbed shoulders with the Punjabi poet Sutinder Singh Noor, and another bringing together the Jnanpith-winning Assamese writer Indira Goswami with the Sahitya Akademi Award–winning Sindhi writer Moti Prakash; and "breakout sessions" conducted by eminent writers in their own languages (thirteen Indian languages were represented). The range and quality of the talent on offer was matched by the breathtaking level of accomplishment on display; it would be like having Saul Bellow, Toni Morrison, John Updike, Philip Roth, Edward Albee, and Don de Lillo all addressing a seminar on American literature in New Delhi.

Indian writing in English was somewhat more modestly represented. I was privileged to be billed as the "main speaker" for a panel discussion on "unity, difference, and history" in Indian literature, with the Akademi's Dr. Narang presiding, and legends like "M. T." and Kambar on the podium alongside — an honor underscored by the presence in the audience of twenty of India's greatest writers and one former prime minister (the polylingual and highly literate P. V. Narasimha Rao). I offered my thoughts on the authenticity of English as a valid language to express the Indian sensibility, arguing that language is ultimately a vehicle, not a destination. To be greeted afterward by two maestros of Hindi writing, Kamleshwar and Manohar Shyam Joshi, with a request for my text so that they could write me a rejoinder, capped my day. (The rejoinder, alas, never came.)

The obligations of my UN life during the first weekend of the annual General Assembly (the event that had brought Prime Minister Vajpayee to New York) prevented me from attending as many of the events as I would have wished, but it was clear that the tireless Dr. Jayaraman had a hit on his hands. The poetry *mushairas* were inevitably the biggest successes, but the quality of the seminar discussions was high. To listen to M. T. Vasudevan Nair describing the Keralite's deep-rooted love of books — "copying texts neatly and artistically was a very common and dignified pastime for middle-class housewives until the first quarter of the last century" — was both instructive and delightful. To hear Harprasad Das, a senior civil servant as well as poet, talk about how the Mahabharata served as a common source of inspiration for both himself and me was stimulating (I was glad he did not draw other parallels between the bureaucratic responsibilities from which both of us have sought to escape in our writing!).

One intervention that I found particularly striking was that of the Kannada poet, playwright, and filmmaker Kambar, who argued that the Indian cultural sensibility was marked by its nonlinear notion of time: "Time is not a controlled sequence of events in our minds, but an amalgamation of all events, past to present." Against the Western notion of "history," Kambar posited a view of "many ages and many worlds," including the mythic, constituting the Indian sense of present reality. Krishna's lesson to Arjuna on the Kurukshetra battlefield, Kambar argued, is not remote for us; that is why the frenzied mobs in Ayodhya cannot be persuaded by those (like me) who want them to leave the past alone. (The intellectual who says to the Bajrang Dal thug, "Leave the past where it is," is confronted by the Hindu sage who replies, "The past is here.")

Kambar went on to challenge the notion that the "lack of historical consciousness is a shortcoming," and declared that it was only an intellectual surrender to the British that led Indians to "consider living outside history an insult." We imitate the West in creating museums to house the relics of our past, whereas traditionally we have lived with our past in our daily present. This British notion of history forces us, Kambar said, to see our own literature through a distorted perspective. We are obsessed with the "original" nature of historic texts and with the need to separate them from later interpolations. Instead of swallowing the Western notion of the integrity of a text and its sole author, we ought to celebrate the way in which Indians continually told and retold the Mahabharata, adding to it and modifying it. It is a matter of pride, Kambar declared, "that an entire country has collectively created the epic over a period of ten thousand years."

This was the point I had myself sought to make in reinventing the Mahabharata myself in my satirical *Great Indian Novel*. At least from 400 B.C. to A.D. 400, we know, the epic was constantly being retold in countless versions around the country. Why did we stop retelling it? And why should we not continue retelling our stories — even in New York?

# 23

# The Poets of Protocol

IT MAY SURPRISE THOSE WITH A DIM VIEW OF DIPLOMACY to learn that Pablo Neruda's intriguing combination of poetry and diplomacy (writing poetry while stationed in an assortment of posts from Colombo to Barcelona and, as ambassador, in France) was far from unique. The late, great Mexican poet Octavio Paz was not only a remarkably popular ambassador to India but used his time there to write marvelous prose and poetry about the country, notably the brilliant *The Monkey Grammarian*. (However, his final ode to Indian civilization, *In Light of India*, was written well after his service in Delhi.)

Paz and Neruda both won the Nobel Prize for Literature, and no one would argue that they weren't greater litterateurs than diplomats. But they were preceded to Stockholm by the 1960 Nobel laureate St. John Perse, the nom de plume of one of the greatest French poets, who was also, as Marie-René Auguste Alexis Saint-Léger Léger, one of his country's most illustrious diplomats — something that could not, strictly speaking, be said of either Neruda or Paz.

Indeed, if he hadn't written a single line of verse, Léger would be remembered as a legendary figure at the quai d'Orsay. A career diplomat since 1904, he became one of his country's most highly respected poets while mounting the hierarchy of his profession. He was made secretary-general of the French Foreign Ministry in 1933, only to be dismissed by the collaborationist Vichy government in 1940. Léger escaped daringly to the United States, where he advised FDR on French affairs; during the war his books were burned and banned in Nazi-occupied France, and Vichy stripped him of his French citizenship. This was restored upon liberation in 1945, and French diplomats still speak of him with reverence. But his literary standing was no less eminent. As a visionary poet of rare distinction, St.-John Perse was regarded so highly that no less a figure than T. S. Eliot translated him into English; his Swedish translator was the United Nations' highly literary secretary-general, Dag Hammarskjold.

Amazingly enough, the Nobelist after St. John Perse was also a diplomat. The 1961 laureate was the Yugoslav Ivo Andric, a master craftsman (often compared to Tolstoy) whose great historical novels of Bosnia, especially *The Bridge on the Drina* and *The Chronicles of Travnik*, enjoyed a modest revival during the horrors of the Balkan wars in the 1990s. Andric was his country's minister (the senior diplomat, one rank below ambassador) in Berlin when war broke out in 1939, and spent much of the period of the war (with his country under German occupation) under house arrest in Belgrade. Today the country he represented as a diplomat no longer exists, but at least three countries — Bosnia-Herzegovina, Croatia, and Serbia — are proud to lay claim to him as a vital part of their literary patrimony.

Four diplomats winning Nobel Prizes for Literature is a remarkable enough statistic, but the list overlooks other fine writer-diplomats of unarguable quality. The French playwright, poet, and essayist Paul Claudel was a diplomat of distinction, serving as his country's ambassador to Belgium, Japan, and the United States, and is widely regarded today as one of the most important figures in French Catholic literature. France's former foreign minister, Dominique de Villepin, whose diplomatic postings included New Delhi, is a superb poet and essayist, who famously worked on his poems while jet-setting around the world from one crisis spot to the next. The British diplomat Lawrence Durrell wrote hilarious accounts of diplomatic life, but he is better remembered for his haunting Alexandria Quartet, four novels published between 1957 and 1960 that won him the highest literary reputation. The Mexican writer-diplomat Carlos Fuentes turned his postings in the United States to advantage in his perceptive evocations of both country's cultures, notably in *The Old Gringo*. The Sri Lankan diplomat Ediriweera Sarachchandra served his country as ambassador in Paris while producing both novels and plays of great repute in his native land. An unusual double features Indran Amirthanayagam, the Sri Lankan–American poet who served in his adopted country's consulate in Madras, and whose late father Guy, an ambassador of Sri Lanka himself, authored two well-reviewed novels.

Africa has been a rich source of literary diplomacy — no surprise to those familiar with the talents of that continent's sophisticated elite. The poet and novelist (*No Bride Price*) David Rubadiri served Malawi twice as its ambassador to the United Nations, with a long stint as an academic in exile in between. The UN also hosted Ghana's Kofi Awonoor, a novelist and poet who spearheaded the organization's fight against apartheid. Cameroon's Ferdinand Oyono rose to the rank of foreign minister but is better known in his own country as a novelist (*The Old Man and the Medal*). Perhaps the finest all-round talent was that of Davidson Nicol of Sierra Leone, who in addition to being his country's leading diplomat (serving as high commissioner to London and permanent representative to the United Nations) was a writer, poet, scientist, and all-round Renaissance man. (I am greatly indebted to my friend Olara Otunnu, Uganda's former foreign minister and a brilliant intellectual himself — though not yet a novelist! — for bringing these distinguished figures to my attention.)

The Indian diplomatic service is hardly an exception to this remarkable tradition. My good friend the late Nina Sibal, who served the country with great distinction and elegance in postings as varied as Cairo and Paris, wrote two fine novels, of which *Yatra* deserves a new generation of readers. The Kerala novelist Mohana Chandran, many of whose best-sellers have been turned into successful Malayalam movies, lived a double life during his long diplomatic career as B. M. C. Nayar. The Ministry of External Affairs' able spokesman, Navtej Sarna, has authored a well-received first novel, *We Weren't Lovers Like That,* and promises more. (Often, those who are good with words in one way are likely to be good with them in another.) The young diplomat Tiru Murti, who has just concluded a successful tour of duty in Washington as a close aide to ambassador Lalit Mansingh, published a very good first novel before the end of his tenure.

Are diplomats uniquely suited — provided they have the gift to begin with — to be good creative writers? My friend and former United Nations colleague Jayantha Dhanapala, a former Sri Lankan ambassador in Washington who is now his government's envoy in the ongoing peace process, certainly thinks so. He argues that the professional diplomat, like the sensitive writer, has to be able to mix with both elites and masses; be firmly rooted in his own culture while open to the experience of others; have inner resources to fall back upon in coping with the isolation of a foreign posting (what Auden called "this nightmare of public solitude"). And most tellingly, as Dhanapala put it in a 1997 lecture, diplomats see creative writing as an escape valve for their professional compromises and frustrations — "an act of expiation for the bruising of the soul they have experienced in their working life." The alternative, for less talented diplomats, has often been alcohol.

# 24

# The Critic as Cosmetologist

SOME YEARS AGO THE ACERBIC BRITISH LABOUR PARTY parliamentarian Denis Healey compared an attack on him by Tory chancellor of the exchequer Geoffrey Howe to being "savaged by a dead sheep." He came to mind one day in 2000, when a press clipping from home revealed that I had just been cuddled by a sharp-clawed minx. Or clawed by a cuddly one: it is usually difficult for the victim to tell.

You see, I had spent a pleasant morning that January in Chennai, the erstwhile Madras, in the company of the members of what is still defiantly called the Madras Book Club, in an atmosphere as warm as the air-conditioning at the five-star hotel was frigid. The literati who had invited me to address them were a highly accomplished lot, including novelists, short-story writers, journalists, editors, and a generous sprinkling of professional reviewers, many for the estimable *Indian Review of Books*, whose publisher, Mr. K. S. Padmanabhan, had put together the event. Among this special breed was a certain generously endowed lady whose wittily ungenerous reviews I had often enjoyed, even on the one occasion her barbs were directed against me. I made the mistake of telling her so when we were introduced.

The morning went well, if the comments of the participants were to be believed, and it was topped off by a splendid lunch. The lady in question proposed a vote of thanks, upon which she and I were roundly applauded. A few days later, however, I received my unjust desserts: a scurrilous piece in an orange-hued rag by the lady herself. It began ominously enough, if you know the genre: "Shashi Tharoor is the epitome of the intellectual as an object of desire." Beware of lavish first sentences from usually tart pens: the acid will flow soon thereafter. It did — in the very next sentence: "He's packaged himself so exquisitely he could have himself stamped 'Made in India' and sold at Macy's."

There followed a somewhat lengthy disquisition on my attire — "a gold-bordered off-white Kerala style mundu . . . with a long blue striped cotton kurta" — in terms that would have had any self-respecting feminist howling in rage if it had been applied to the attire of a female novelist. (Women are understandably furious at their outfits being described as if they were integral to people's perception of their work, and it's no prettier when it's a woman doing it to a man.) The lady then speculated on my kurta's provenance: "Fabindia?" For the record, it was from a modest pavement stall on Gariahat Road in Calcutta that has since been demolished by that city's urban-renewal zealots. Also, its stripes were green and gold, not blue, but then color blindness is not apparently a disqualification for sartorial commentary in our more expensive papers.

THE CRITIC AS COSMETOLOGIST

The lady didn't stop there. "Even the folds of his mundu-veshti hang in unnaturally straight lines," she opines. "He would be laughed off the streets of Calicut if he were to appear in such a garb. As everyone knows, the Keralite has innumerable ways of twitching up and hitching his mundu around his waist and furling it down as he walks and talks. Tharoor wears his like a ball-gown." Now I have no idea how ball gowns are worn, never having needed to sport one, but this attack would have been below the belt, had I needed to wear a belt. I have no idea of the social circles in which the lady waddles, but we Keralites hitch our *mundus* or *lungis* up in casual settings, when fording a paddy field or chatting with friends, never at a formal occasion, where it would be considered disrespectful and improper. I have spoken at many a Kerala function at which *mundus* were worn by the participants, and they always hung in straight lines. As one who has donned nothing but *mundus* and *lungis* during innumerable stays at my ancestral village, I doubt I have anything to learn from a Chennai socialite about how to dress comfortably in rural India; but one look at her ample proportions was enough to explain to me why she might indeed consider straight lines unnatural.

And yet that wasn't the end of the ad hominem dissection of this beleaguered novelist. "His haircut is a dead giveaway," she declares. "It's fashionably shaggy and American preppy, falling in strands over his noble brow, with not a drop of coconut oil." Now that's hilarious. Anyone who has known me since I was old enough to give my own instructions to a barber knows that I've always worn my hair that way — in high school in Calcutta, college in Delhi, and on visits to Kerala. The haircut in question, which the optically gifted lady imagined to be American, had actually been done at a dusty saloon in the Coimbatore suburb of Kovaipudur, as far removed as possible from the fashionable origins it was supposedly a "dead giveaway" for.

But enough of all this: what exactly is the lady's point? It is, of course, that dreaded nemesis of every Indo-Anglian writer: the denizen of Desi-dom challenging the authenticity of the NRI. It little matters that friends from thirty years back remember me debating on my school team in a flaming cotton kurta with my unruly hair flopping over my face: for me to stand up and do so today, as I have always done, is not acceptable to the lady and her ilk because it does not pass her acid test of what is really, truly Indian. For her, my sin is not that I have traveled too far from my roots, but that I haven't traveled far enough to please her. Had I come to the Madras Book Club in jeans and a sweatshirt, or in a pinstriped suit, no doubt she would have drawn the same conclusions from the opposite evidence. But it is time we all averred that literary mavens have no more right than Hindutva chauvinists to declare who or what is authentically Indian. There are many voices and accents engaged in our national conversation. The pun-spouting Stephanian is much an Indian as the dhoti-clad *dehati*, and the Stephanian does not become less — or more — of an Indian if he dons the *dehati's* dhoti. No more than the *dehati* ceases to be Indian if he pulls on a pair of Levi's.

These are, the lady will tell us, platitudes. It's a pity she made it necessary to repeat them.

# 25

# The Cultural Geography of Criticism

IT TOOK AN EDITORIAL IN A PUBLICATION I READ, respected, and wrote for — the late lamented *Indian Review of Books* — to prompt me to break a long-standing, if self-imposed, rule.

I had made it a point not to discuss reviews of my own books in any of my own writing. This is not because I am excessively modest, or unduly burdened by a sense of authorial propriety; it is simply that I believe that a book, once published, has to make its own way in the world. Authors do not like bad reviews any more than parents like to hear criticisms of their children, and the temptation to lash out at the most unfair of them is great. But as a reader I am aware that reactions to fiction are inevitably subjective. A reviewer's dislike of a particular book says at least as much about the reviewer as it does about the book.

I have therefore been content to let reviews of my books stand unchallenged, even when — as sadly happens too often in India — the reviewer bases his or her judgments on a partial reading, or a willful misreading, of the book. This policy has, I must admit, been made easier by the fact that I have been lucky enough to have had far more positive, indeed enthusiastic, reviews around the world for my books than unfavorable ones.

But an *IRB* editorial obliged me to break my silence. Entitled "Some Thoughts on Reviewing," it discussed two reviews of my 1992 novel *Show Business* — an assault on the book as "irritatingly superficial" by Shobha Dé in the *IRB*, and a front-page accolade by William Boyd in the *New York Times Book Review*, which I am told was the first such tribute accorded by the *Times* to an Indian writer. After quoting a paragraph from each review, the anonymous editorialist commented that "such widely disparate views about the same book, and in fact about its essential thrust, cannot but fail to raise several questions in the average reader's mind." Praising the credentials and the integrity of both reviewers, the editorialist wonders whether the difference is that one is an Indian and the other American (Boyd is in fact British, but let us let that pass). Can "a critic from one culture," the *IRB* asks, "wholly appreciate the nuances in the writings from another culture?"

That is a fair question — I concede that no foreigner can get as much out of my *Great Indian Novel* as an Anglophone Indian can — and yet a misleading one. If the attitude implicit in that query were carried to its logical extreme, Gabriel García Márquez could not be given the Nobel Prize by a bunch of Swedes, Salman Rushdie could not be banned by an Iranian Ayatollah, and the Sahitya Akademi might as well wind up, since no Indian would be able to appreciate its translations of novels from other Indian languages. The entire point about literature is that, while it may emerge from a specific culture, it must speak to readers of other linguistic and cultural traditions, for what endures in good writing is not culture-specific. We read literature from other cultures all the time; and we do so because literature, whether or not from a society we know, serves to illuminate and deepen our appreciation of the human condition.

But as a writer — an Indian writer — I object equally to the notion that a reviewer's individual judgment can be vindicated by his or her passport. The idea that Ms. Dé's attack on *Show Business* can be justified by the fact that, in the *IRB* editorialist's words, she "is an Indian, with a more than adequate knowledge of the Indian background, who finds the book wanting in substance and depth" is to me a dangerous one. (Let us leave aside the temptingly obvious riposte that though Ms. Dé has been accused of many sins, an excess of "substance and depth" has never been one of them.) India has never been a country where nationality has been a determinant of opinion. In literature as in politics, there are as many opinions as there are Indians. There are Indians who don't like *Show Business*, and there are Indians who do: I have had excellent reviews from several of them, as well as letters and conversations with innumerable readers whose Indianness didn't appear to obstruct their appreciation of the novel.

Equally pernicious is the suggestion that William Boyd's praise — and by implication that of the many other reviewers in the West who admired the book, including the *Washington Post*'s eminent Jonathan Yardley, who picked it as one of the four best books of the year — is somehow diluted by the fact they are foreigners. Boyd (*An Ice-Cream War, Brazzaville Beach,* and three Booker Prize nominations behind him) features on every critic's list of the top three Englishmen writing fiction today; he doesn't know me, has no ax to grind, and indeed has a formidable reputation to protect, one that could only be damaged by careless praise for an unworthy novel. Much as some of us might like it, Western writers have better things to do than to spend their time casting ignorant kudos on Indian books.

So — to return to the entirely legitimate concerns of the *IRB* editorial — how are we to evaluate such widely disparate reviews? The answer is of more than passing interest, since the need for a serious reviewing tradition in India is one that concerns every Indian writer. It seems to me that the answer lies in the reviews themselves. On what does the reviewer base his or her judgment? Is the reviewer's "knowledge" an asset or a handicap — in other words, does the reviewer bring too many preconceptions and prejudices to the book? Are the criticisms couched in intemperate, wholly subjective terms, or do they cite evidence from the book that could convince an uncommitted reader?

Ms. Dé's review speaks eloquently for itself, even in the passage quoted in the editorial. "Yes, Hindi films are full of cardboard characters, but do we need to *read* about them . . . ?" she asks (emphasis added). No one needs to read about anything, but does the reviewer ask what the novelist has tried to do with these characters? Adjectives like "tedious" and "prudish" may reflect Ms. Dé's standards rather than the culture's; some Indian reviewers went the other way, criticizing the book as airy and salacious, and the *London Sunday*

*Times* reviewer, the novelist Jonathan Coe, declared that it was "an enormously funny and enjoyable novel which has never for a moment been frivolous." What critics like Boyd, Yardley, and others found worth praising were the "architecture" of the novel, its narrative structure, its attempt to weave larger themes (reality and illusion, dharma and accountability, the place of films in our society and of our society in our films) into an entertaining story. None of these factors even found a mention in the negative Indian reviews of *Show Business*. Had the Indian critics acknowledged the author's endeavor and then found that the book fell short in the attempt, their criticisms could have been taken seriously; but when the reviewer's reading of the book is so superficial that it fails even to notice what the author has tried to do, it undermines the worth of the review.

Writers need bad reviews almost as much as they welcome good ones. It keeps us honest to be told when we've gone wrong. But reviewers must learn to tackle books on their own terms, not the reviewers'. Rise to a book and find it wanting, by all means; but do the author the courtesy of reading it first and thinking about it before reacting. That is the only way we will attain the high critical standards that remain the best guarantee of a lively — and ever-improving — literary tradition.

# 26

# How Not to Deal with a Bad Review

I HAVE RECENTLY BEEN INVOLVED in a minor literary controversy in the pages of the *New York Times*, whose editors felt compelled to acknowledge to their readers that the author of what is politely called a "mixed" review of my recent book *Nehru: The Invention of India* had himself received a mixed review from me some years earlier for one of his books. Turnabout, to upend a cliché, was not considered fair play.

The episode was trivial, but it reminded me of a far more entertaining incident in the same pages a decade earlier, involving Norman Mailer. Short, strong, and beer-bellied, with a pugnacious thrust of jaw and wiry gray hair, the eminent novelist (*The Naked and the Dead*), biographer (*Marilyn*), reporter (*The Armies of the Night*), and polemicist (*The Prisoner of Sex*) is a considerable presence on the American literary scene. Boozy, brawling, and bold, reviled by feminists for his attitude to women, excoriated by the Right for his opposition to the Vietnam War, Mailer is one author who is as much read about as read. The former enfant terrible of American letters has, in a turbulent career, married and divorced a succession of women, drunk himself silly in public, marched in raucous protest demonstrations, run (unsuccessfully) for mayor of New York, and bibulously engaged in public fisticuffs.

Criticizing the work of such a combative figure is hardly a low-risk occupation. Other authors might react to an unjust review with the attitude of the old Persian proverb, "When the caravan passes, the dogs bark" (for why should a caravan be distracted by every barking dog?). But not Norman Mailer. In the early 1990s reviewers trashed Mailer's long-awaited magnum opus, *Harlot's Ghost*, a 1,334-page novel about the CIA and the American psyche that ended, ominously enough, with the words *To be continued*. The London *Sunday Times*'s Peter Kemp, a notoriously trenchant demolition expert, called the novel "the appalling manifestation of a defunct talent." But the review that really got Mailer's goat, perhaps because it appeared in the one publication that matters most to American writers, was that of John Simon in the *New York Times Book Review*.

Simon, better known as a theater critic, found *Harlot's Ghost* an "arbitrary, lopsided, lumpy novel that outstays its welcome." Mailer's "hang-ups are too naked, puerile, perverse," wrote Simon, adding that "what he lacks is [a good] editor." Worse has been written by reviewers — and some of Simon's 2,500-word critique was even complimentary — but Mailer blew a gasket. He stormed into the offices of the *New York Times*, demanding — and obtaining — a meeting with the managing editor of the paper and the editor of the book review section. Simon, he alleged, was biased against him: Mailer had apparently described Simon years ago as being "as predictable in his critical reactions as a headwaiter." Simon, in return, had reviewed a play starring Mailer's daughter Kate, and called her a "rotten" actress "who mugs and simpers." Mailer demanded that the *Times* grant him the right of reply.

Somewhat to the astonishment of the American literary establishment, the *Times* said yes. Though Simon protested not only that he stood by the review but that its only defect was that "it was too kind," the *Times* gave Mailer the space for a 1,500-word response. This repeated the author's accusations against the reviewer, and added the delectable snippet that he had challenged Simon, after the critic's attack on his daughter, to meet him outside if he was a man of honor. But the burden of Mailer's charge was that Simon had misrepresented himself as someone who "had a rather neutral relationship" with the author, and therefore could be counted upon to do a fair review. In fact, Mailer said, Simon's reviews of two of Mailer's earlier books had been so venomous that he should have been disqualified from reviewing this one.

Simon replied, somewhat pompously, that "it is characteristic of Norman Mailer's cult of personality (instead of cultivation of craft) that the attempted refutation of my review addresses itself to just about everything except the review itself." The then-editor chimed in that Simon "wrote a fair and balanced review that met the standards of this newspaper." But, she added, "normally the *Book Review* would not assign a book to a critic who had frequently disparaged its author's work, or one who had a personal relationship, positive or negative, with the author." (Those standards, incidentally, are widely upheld in America but completely ignored in England, where books are usually reviewed by friends or enemies of the author, and reviews are often the occasion for either mutual back-scratching or the settling of scores. My own reviewer is British-based.)

There are writers who believe that any publicity is good publicity — as one publisher put it, "people will remember that they've read about your book long after they forget what they'd read about it." So Mailer's attack on Simon, even if it drew attention to the negative review of his book, fueled more interest in it. Some uncharitable observers saw the entire episode as an attempt by the larger-than-life author to revive his novel's flagging fortunes in the nether regions of the best-seller lists. If so, it didn't work; *Harlot's Ghost* sank rapidly off the charts.

Predictably enough, the Mailer-Simon exchange itself became the subject of further polemics. Letters flooded in to the *Times*, and the strongest arguments went against Mailer. "If you're going to pander to Norman Mailer's wounded ego," one reader asked the *Times*, "why not save time and trouble in the future and simply let Mr. Mailer review his own books? He clearly enjoys writing about himself in the third person, and assigning him the review would make a lengthy rebuttal unnecessary (though Mr. Mailer would, of course, still be free to threaten himself with physical injury if he came to doubt his own fairness). Not only would this be a service to Mr. Mailer, it would be a service to readers, who could then sample Mr. Mailer's writing style before committing themselves to 1,300-plus pages." As for himself, the reader went on, he had planned to buy *Harlot's Ghost,* but "after slogging through the overdone prose of Mr. Mailer's counterattack" had decided his $30 would be better spent on beer.

All of which is not very encouraging to any author who may be contemplating assaulting a nasty reviewer, even if only in print. The moral of the story, it seems to me as one who has both written and received reviews, is that it is better to leave well enough alone. A review, good or bad, is a transient thing; a book, if it was worth writing, will endure long after the review is forgotten. Let the dogs bark; the caravan must move on.

## 27

# Elegy for a Literary Monument

IN 2003, LITERATE INDIANS CELEBRATED the 125th anniversary of the magnificent newspaper for which I write regularly, the *Hindu*. But amid the celebrations another, sadder anniversary of a print publication passed almost unnoticed. September 2003 marked the second anniversary of the demise of a remarkable venture in Indian publishing, the *Indian Review of Books*, just one issue short of what would have been its tenth birthday. I remember looking forward with anticipation to what the *IRB* would have made of my novel *Riot*, which was slated to have been reviewed in the magazine's September 2001 issue. But the August issue arrived with an editorial headlined "End of a Dream": "It is with a deep sense of sadness," the magazine wrote, "that we announce the closure of *IRB*." India's best literary journal had finally been defeated by the hard mathematics of the market.

Founded by K. S. Padmanabhan of the highly respected Madras publishing house East-West Books and backed financially largely by his own resources, the *IRB* had carved a niche for itself among discerning readers — but not, alas, among advertisers. The magazine was distinguished by some of the best writing about books one could find in India. Its contributors, including some of the finest minds in the country, eschewed both the jargon-laden self-importance of academic journals and the superficial plot summaries of the popular press, offering instead the thoughtful insights and provocative judgments that true book lovers value everywhere. One did not have to like everything that appeared between its covers to appreciate the worth of the endeavor, in a country that has only recently begun to engage in a grand national conversation about literature. I welcomed the arrival in the mail of each issue with genuine excitement: I knew it would provide both instruction and delight.

"Are we aborning, like Chesterton's donkey, at some moment when the moon is blood?" the editors had asked themselves in their inaugural issue. They knew they were undertaking a risk. But they saw that book publishing had finally come of age in India, and they felt that a good review journal would serve to bring "book and reader together." India was at last ready for a *swadeshi* equivalent to the *New York Review of Books* or *London Review of Books.* Most of India's major English-language publishing houses were not much older than the *IRB;* some, indeed, had come into existence since its founding. One would have expected the two sister professions to make common cause. Publishers need well-informed readers, and one might have imagined they would want to support a high-quality literary magazine in order to enhance their own sales. But their advertising was minimal;

one could turn page after page of *IRB* without finding the prose interrupted by an ad.

Advertising is the oxygen of any newspaper. The first reality of the "free press" is that you must not take the adjective literally, since it is anything but free: there are always bills to be paid that vastly exceed what the subscription price can bring in. The *IRB*'s subscription lists barely crossed the five-figure mark, and with modest advertising revenue, the economics of magazine publishing meant that the *IRB* was losing some fifty thousand rupees — just over a thousand dollars — an issue. (Note to idealistic students: economics always trumps literature.) After ten years of struggle, Mr. Padmanabhan and his well-wishers came to the reluctant conclusion that the *IRB* was never going to be able to pay for itself. Even the most generous blood donor cannot sustain an indefinite hemorrhage, and Mr. Padmanabhan, the mainstay of the Madras Book Club and a man with books in his blood, ultimately had to stanch the flow.

Today, two years later, there is still no adequate substitute for the *IRB*. The *Book Review*, published in Delhi, miraculously seems to keep afloat, but it makes fewer concessions to nonacademic readers than the *IRB*, and too many of its reviews seem to be written by professors for the delectation of other professors. *Biblio* is often more readable, but its publication schedule over the years has been erratic, and its choice of subject matter idiosyncratic. Neither has ever covered the range of books that the *IRB* managed to treat in each issue — novels, serious nonfiction, travel and cookery books, children's stories. The loss to India's readers is still enduring.

And yet — as the old song asked, does it have to be this way? Surely there must be, in our newly globalizing economy, some business house that can afford half a lakh of rupees a month — not just to support a good cause, but to reach an educated clientele? It costs one of our multinational corporations more than that amount to produce a few seconds of one of their television commercials. The editorial staff and infrastructure of the *IRB* are still in place at East-West, along with a network of willing contributors and even the old subscription lists. All they need is a benefactor. I am sure I would not be the only literate Indian consumer to say that if Coke or Pepsi came to the rescue of *IRB*, I would gladly switch my thirst-driven allegiance to them. A brand that sustains a magazine of ideas has a greater claim on my loyalty than one that is endorsed by a cricketer or an actor.

So here's the challenge to any corporate chieftain who happens to be reading this. Take on the resurrection of the country's best book review magazine. Put your name on the cover if you must; give yourself a few ad pages in return for the funds; but let the editors continue to celebrate and promote the joy of reading. An *IRB* may never make it to a 125th anniversary, but they deserve better than to have fallen before their tenth.

# 28

# Why the Yeti Brings Hope to a
# Land without Snow

W HILE WAITING FOR GOOD NEWS that might reverse the
demise of that splendid literary publication, the *In-dian Review of Books*, I am pleased to report positive devel-opments on another literary front. In late 2003 I heard from
two different correspondents about exciting new ventures
that suggest that there is still life and vitality on the Indian
publishing scene.

The first piece of news comes from my home state, Ker-ala, where a group of young poets and writers in Kozhikode
(Calicut) — not heretofore considered a bastion of English-language publishing in India — have launched a new im-print, Yeti Books. Their logo is the famous footprint of the
Abominable Snowman, not a figure commonly associated
with tropical Calicut, but symbolic both of the leap of imag-ination they have undertaken and the "barefoot" nature of
their enterprise. I have four Yeti volumes before me as I
write this column, and they make an excellent impression.
They are attractively designed, carefully proofread, and

handsomely printed and bound; there is none of the shoddiness one associates with the many amateur literary operations that have emerged from small-town India.

The quality of Yeti's writers is equally impressive. Poetry appears to be their forté, which is not surprising considering that the imprint's principal founder, Thachom Poyil Rajeevan, is himself a poet of some standing in both Malayalam and English. Dom Moraes heads the Yeti list, and Anita Nair, whose fiction has already made its mark, emerges with a debut collection of poems that, Rajeevan proudly informs me, is already in its second edition.

I asked Rajeevan by e-mail for information about the background of his associates and himself, the challenges they have faced in getting their project off the ground, how they were managing financially, and so on. Whether out of Rajeevan's modesty or the vagaries of electronic communication, I do not have answers to these questions. I can only assume that Yeti is a labor of love and that its financial survival requires the support and dedication of distributors, libraries — and above all, readers. The niche that Yeti is seeking to carve out for itself — of high-quality poetry and literary fiction, some of it in translation — is not necessarily remunerative. But the fact that there are young men and women in India prepared to dedicate their creative energies to this sort of publishing augurs well. The foreword to Rajeevan's own books of poems, *He Who Was Gone Thus*, reveals that he is a public relations officer of the University of Calicut who writes in his spare time. That the University of Calicut harbors such talent in its midst is itself a priceless public relations asset of which I hope the university's administrators are proud.

The second new venture is the development of a series of school textbooks at Oxford University Press, on the theme "Peace and Value Education for National Integration." *National integration* is a term we were used to hearing much more in earlier times, but in the aftermath of the Gujarat atrocities it has acquired new meaning and urgency. The OUP series editor, Mini Krishnan, has already stewarded the publication of a well-regarded series of translations from various Indian languages into English, but this new project has a special resonance for those who believe that Indian publishing can contribute to the development of an integrative national consciousness.

Her publishing philosophy, Ms. Krishnan explains, is to produce educational materials that serve to remove prejudice and instill peace and understanding in young children — and to do so across the communal divide that some politicians have been so eager to foment. The series' subjects will include material designed to enhance intercommunal relationships, the need to understand human differences, and related themes. The writers will be Indians of Hindu, Muslim, and Christian backgrounds, and the books will be designed to serve not only as textbooks but also as workbooks, so that children can learn for themselves, and process through their own minds, the values of peace, tolerance, and coexistence without which "national integration" will remain a hollow slogan.

I do not know either Thachom Poyil Rajeevan or Mini

Krishnan well, and I have no commercial or professional interest in the success of their ventures. But both seem to me to exemplify something of great value to the future of India. They represent the spirit of those who are not content to take the world as it is, who have ideas of how to improve the life they see around them, and who are untiring in their pursuit of these ideas. By choosing the far from lucrative field of publishing (literary publishing in Rajeevan's case, textbook publishing in Krishnan's) they have also sought to devote their creative energies to an activity that is beleaguered everywhere in the world and desperately in need of nurturing in India.

So more power to their pens (or, these days, to their keyboards). May Yeti's handsome volumes of poetry stir thousands of souls and make their idealistic publishers a profit, and may OUP's national integration series (still on the drawing boards) move millions of young minds toward integration and away from hatred. And (to remind well-heeled readers of my earlier appeal) may the *Indian Review of Books* be revived to review them both.

# 29

# How *Riot* Nearly Caused a Riot

I CAN SEE THE DOUBLE STANDARD HERE," the Indian actress, activist, and parliamentarian Shabana Azmi snapped. "Muslims say they are proud to be Muslim, Christians say they are proud to be Christian, Sikhs say they are proud to be Sikh, and Hindus say they are proud to be . . . secular."

All right, Shabana Azmi didn't really say it. Not as Shabana Azmi: she was on stage in New York's New School University auditorium, reading lines I wrote in my novel *Riot*, which had been adapted for the occasion by the American director Michael Johnson-Chase. And she was playing the angry Hindu chauvinist Ram Charan Gupta, a character as far removed from Shabana Azmi's own perceptions of communal realities in India as it is possible to be.

But that was the whole point of the event. Its principal organizers, the Indo-American Arts Council, wanted to create a piece of literary theater in New York that went to the heart of the current communal divide in India. The reading gave voice to the different viewpoints articulated by the characters in the book (who are caught up in a fictional riot on the same issues that underlay the recent carnage in the Indian state of Gujarat), in order to set the stage for a discussion with the audience of communal issues in India and the recent tragic violence in Gujarat in particular.

So the novel was adapted to a staged reading for four characters, whose contending views of the nature of Indian nationhood would play off each other dramatically. Shabana Azmi agreed to lend her considerable prestige to the event. So did the wonderful thespian and culinary celebrity Madhur Jaffrey and the pugnaciously articulate *Wall Street Journal* editorialist Tunku Varadarajan. I added my own voice to the list, reading the part of a hard-drinking, hard-swearing Sikh police officer whose family had suffered in the 1984 anti-Sikh riots in Delhi but who still affirmed a vision for himself in building a pluralist India from which no group would feel excluded.

To share the experience with personalities of this caliber was a real privilege. And it was made more so by the antics of a fringe group of Hindu chauvinist agitators, calling themselves (a nice Orwellian touch, this) "Indian-Americans for Truth and Fairness in the Media," which embarked on a hate campaign against Shabana Azmi and, incidentally, myself in the weeks leading up to the reading. But their attempts to stir up hostility to the event, by a hysterical and somewhat indiscriminate series of e-mails asking people to protest outside the hall (one of which I even received myself!) backfired; it simply prompted a number of secular Indians to organize a counterdemonstration. So while the four of us declaimed to a full house of five hundred, a noisier scene took place outside the auditorium. The slogans of hate were drowned out by the chants of the anticommunal groups. Soon enough, the frustrated zealots stopped their sloganeering, and turned their backs on the counter-protestors.

It may seem odd that this little drama was enacted thousands of miles from the India with whose urgent realities it was concerned. But the passions of Indian expatriates acutely mirror the divisions in their homeland. The problem is precisely with those who would turn their backs on dialogue, and that is what the four-member cast stressed in the lively discussion with the (mostly Indian) audience that followed the reading. If we could all understand that — as my novel tries to show — the very pluralism of our arguments is a metaphor for the pluralism of India itself, we might again be able to find ways to live together as we have done for hundreds of years. That is why it was important that a Muslim secularist like Shabana Azmi should voice the impassioned rage of Ram Charan Gupta (which she did so well, I found myself remarking, that I was almost convinced myself!). Understanding the point of view of those with whom we profoundly disagree is, of course, the first step toward learning to create a society that manages such disagreement.

The family of a Muslim politician who had been murdered in the Gujarat riots drove for over two hours to New York in order to take part in the discussion after the reading, but arrived late and (unknown to the cast) was not allowed inside by security. So members of the family stood on the street and talked with the demonstrators. "What was remarkable," one of the protestors said, "was that they spoke without hatred and anger, only a great deal of sadness and grief." That is the true measure of Indianness — not the hatred and anger of those who want to overturn the injustices of centuries past, but the grief and sadness of those who mourn the loss of justice and harmony in the present, and fear its absence in the future. It is an Indianness being tenuously kept alive by Indian expatriates in America, who hope that the same battle for tolerance will be fought on the more important stage back home.

# IV

## Appropriations

# 30

# With Friends Like These

I WAS NOT PRESENT ON DECEMBER II, 1991, when Salman Rushdie stunned an audience at New York's Columbia University with an unexpected speech about his predicament after nearly three years of hiding. His listeners at Columbia's famous School of Journalism that day had gathered to commemorate the U.S. Bill of Rights; there had been no public announcement of his presence. But as a videotape I have seen of the twenty-minute event reveals, Rushdie's appearance at the podium was electrifying. He emerged onto a dimly lit stage seemingly out of nowhere, as if conjured by one of his own narratorial sleights-of-hand, and not even the sight of the uneasy security guards flanking him inhibited the outbreak of spontaneous applause. The assembled glitterati rose to their feet, as they did again when he finished with the despairing words: "Ladies and gentlemen, the balloon is sinking into the abyss."

It was an extraordinary performance, and a moving one. But in the outpouring of words that have been printed and published in the United States about Rushdie, the writer who described himself to his American listeners as "a lonely Indian immigrant" had become an involuntary totem for a cultural crusade — one on which, had it concerned anyone else, he might have found himself on the other side.

For there was much about his own supporters that Rushdie must have found disturbing. That his problems should have given ammunition to the skinheads and yobs and gutter racists of his adopted country to hurl at other immigrant Muslims. That his defenders included many whose right-wing views on most political matters he would have found far from congenial. That the major piece carried by the august *New York Times* to mark the painful third anniversary of the fatwa was one by the American writer Paul Theroux excoriating Iran as a land of "disgusting" and "barbarous" fanatics with "fatuous laws." Theroux wrote that, on his extensive (and extensively chronicled) travels, he had been confronting every Muslim he met, from taxi drivers to peasants, and "setting them straight" about their "ignorant sentiments." So here we have Salman Rushdie, a writer who has done so much to reclaim the narratives of his own people from interpretations either imperial or imperious, being defended by a man who goes around picking smug quarrels with Muslims. Theroux urged the public to emulate him: if they did so, "I have no doubt that eventually the message will get through, and he will be free." Whether such disingenuous advice was dangerous, insulting, or merely fatuous, Rushdie was ill served by much of this advocacy.

The Iranian-style collar of the shirt Rushdie wore at his Columbia appearance symbolized more than one irony. The foremost British spokesman for the interests and perceptions of Indian Muslims had found himself assailed, persecuted, by his own constituency. And his cause had seen him being appropriated by the West in a clash of cultures that left no room for his own, that of the secular urban subcontinental. Perhaps it was for us, the English-speaking heirs to the same broad tradition, to reclaim Rushdie for ourselves. And certainly for the tribe he has led with such distinction, that of Indian writers in English.

For we were the ones who were deeply and personally diminished by Rushdie's imprisonment — and for all practical purposes, imprisonment is what it was. The irony was all the more intense because, for all of us today who write of Indian experience in the English language, he is the one who lifted the shackles. Not only did he widen our proverbial horizons; he expanded, in his own phrase, the realm of the possible. When I reviewed *Midnight's Children* for the *Singapore Straits Times*, I called it "The Great Indian Novel" (a title I have mischievously reused for less worthy reasons). But the enduring measure of its greatness will always be the number, and sometimes the quality, of those who rushed to follow Salman Rushdie through the wide doors that *Midnight's Children* opened out of the closed compound of "Indo-Anglian" writing.

Before the fatwa, I had never met Salman Rushdie. But when I read *Imaginary Homelands* in 1991 on my way back from a holiday in India that he was no longer free to take, I was moved by the mind and the sensibility to which it testified, and by the enormity of the attempts to silence both. I had read many of Rushdie's essays when they first appeared, including one with which I had vehemently disagreed at the time in print. But to reread them, and to reread them in one binding, was to rediscover Rushdie, as it were, whole; to understand again, only more fully, the values that had shaped him, the rhythms that had quickened his pulse. These were Indian values, the ones most of the readers of my own writings had also been brought up with. And he moved to a rhythm so many of us know intimately — in the words of his favorite lyrics, his *joota* (shoe) may have been Japani but his *dil* (heart) was indubitably Hindustani.

For this reason, Indians who have grown up in the same urban milieu — whatever their views on his specific transgressions — could not afford to distance themselves from Rushdie. The distorted debate over one book could not be allowed to obscure what Rushdie meant to us as a writer of other books. The monstrous injustice to which he has been subjected was an assault on all of us who legitimately take pride in him.

When I argued this case in the *Indian Express* in early 1992 I wrote, with defiant optimism, "It will, of course, be a while before Salman Rushdie can resume something approaching a normal life. But I do believe — and not just because I want to believe — that he will gradually be able to do so. One can see from the joyful affirmations of *Haroun and the Sea of Stories* that he is far from losing faith, and that he does not need strangers to shore his up. But it is vital to tell him that he has touched us, his truest compatriots; that we care, and that we are waiting for him to be restored to all of us, and to the world."

In my first novel I paid Rushdie tribute as one who has

labeled a generation and revolutionized a literature. There were, I was convinced, even greater achievements ahead of him, and I called upon many more Indians to join me in looking forward with hope and anticipation to the works in which he would go forward to claim them. That these works have come, and that he is now free, free above all to return to his beloved — and no longer merely imagined — homeland, is a triumph not only over those who would have silenced him but over those who sought to shackle his genius to their prejudices.

# 31

# From the Bathtub to Bollywood

I T WAS THE FIRST TIME anybody had called me from his
bathtub. At least, it was the first time anybody had told
me he was calling from his bathtub, and it certainly got my
attention.

"I've just been reading the *New York Times* review of
your novel *Show Business*," said Bikramjit ("Blondie") Singh,
"and it sounds great! I want to make a movie of it."

I was a bit taken aback. You haven't read the book yet,
and you want to make a movie out of it? was the first question that came to mind. Or did he want to make a movie of
the review?

"Of course I'll read the book, but I'm sure I'll like it.
The review sounds fabulous. You know, seven people sent
it to me — friends and associates from all over America. A
business partner of mine in New York wrote a note with it.
It just said: Call him! I was reading the review in the bathtub, and I was so excited I just had to call you immediately."

I had never known my prose to have interrupted anyone's ablutions before. I was suitably flattered. "Fine, I'll meet you in New York," I agreed. Then the author in me asserted himself: "But read the book first."

He did. And it left his enthusiasm unimpaired. So Bikramjit ("BJ" to his American friends) and his attractive wife Jeana called on me in New York to persuade me of their credentials to commit my immortal prose to perishable celluloid. BJ was a larger-than-life character, a bearded Sikh who wore his long hair in a ponytail, dressed in a beaded vest, Levi's, and cowboy boots, and spoke like the Indian public schoolboy he had been (Bishop Cotton's, Simla) before he made his adventurous way to America. He was relaxed, garrulous, and engaging, the epitome of the Indian-American entrepreneur. He had just returned from a trip to Mahabalipuram, where he'd persuaded the local stonecutters, heirs to a centuries-old tradition of temple carving, to sculpt statues of Elvis Presley and Madonna for the American market ("They've done Indian gods and goddesses, now they can do an American god and goddess — what's the difference?").

Though based in Marblehead, Massachusetts, BJ had been involved in Bollywood for years. He rattled off the names of a number of productions he'd been associated with (of which *Mr. Natwarlal* was the only title I recognized). I had, as a writer in love with the printed word, never imagined that anything of mine could be filmable. I thought I wrote highly literary fiction, in which the prose style, the metaphors, the subtle allusions, even the very architecture of the novels, were central to what I was trying to convey. How could the multiple narratives of *Show Business,* its interlocking stories of films and filmdom, its shifts in perspective, its political and religious subthemes, translate onto the screen? I was apprehensive, and intrigued.

"Who'll write the screenplay?" I asked. (I had made it clear that, as a result of my responsibilities for United Nations peacekeeping operations in the former Yugoslavia, I could not be involved in any way with the production.)

"I will," replied BJ. "I couldn't trust anyone else to do it. And besides, I'll be faithful to the book."

He was — to begin with. The first draft of his screenplay consisted of almost the entire novel, slightly rearranged but otherwise largely unaltered. I was relieved — until I realized that this draft, if it was ever filmed, would make an eight-hour movie. "I'll have to cut it a bit," BJ admitted.

And so began the saga that transformed my book into his movie, a process every author who has signed away the rights to his work knows only too well, and only too painfully.

The first surprise came when my agent showed me the signed contract that gave BJ the "option" to the book — the usual Hollywood arrangement whereby, for 10 percent of the total fee, the producer retains exclusive rights for a period of time to "develop the property" and search for his funding. The contract was signed "Caliph S. Kahn."

I rang up BJ. "I thought you said you wanted to make the movie." I said. "Who the hell is Caliph S. Kahn?"

"I am," he replied.

"But you told me you're Bikramjit Singh!"

"I am Bikramjit Singh," he responded equably. "BJ to my friends here, Blondie to my friends in Bollywood. But my full name is Caliph Bikramjit Singh Khan, spelt Kahn in the American style. You've written about Indian secularism — how much more secular can you get?"

So he was going to sign the contract as Caliph S. Kahn, write the screenplay as Bikramjit Singh, work in Bombay as Blondie Singh, and direct the movie as B. J. Kahn. "Hope you don't mind," he said disarmingly.

If his wife and the taxman didn't, how could I? I asked my agent whether she was bothered by the multiple identities of the man who'd bought my book. "Naw," she replied. "Happens all the time in Hollywood."

I couldn't help feeling a bit like a father who's given his daughter away and discovers the suitor carries four different driving licenses. What else didn't I know? I wondered, till my agent gave me sage advice.

"You've got to let go," she said. "It's not your book anymore. You've signed the contract. Now it's his project."

And so it was, but in the months to follow I couldn't help indulging my quasi-paternal curiosity about its evolution. BJ raised the funds from a Taiwanese financier based in San Francisco and an Indian-American businessman from Los Angeles. The script began to be whittled down; though the contract didn't call for it, BJ showed me each draft, and I winced as more and more of the novel disappeared from the screenplay. I gamely suggested alternative cuts, feeling like an amputee choosing which of his limbs to surrender to the butcher's knife.

The casting process began: BJ returned from trips to Bombay with stories of the big-name stars who, he said, were practically clamoring to be cast in his film. Chunky Pandey, a bankable name, had agreed to play the hero. "And Mehnaz?"

I asked, referring to the hero's superstar mistress. "That's proving more difficult," BJ replied, "though so-and-so and you-know-who are very interested." (He dropped a couple of names that made me catch my breath.) "But I'm not sure they're quite right for the part. Who would you suggest?"

I hesitantly mentioned that I had rather imagined my Mehnaz as a cross between Zeenat Aman and Parveen Babi. BJ looked at me as if I had spoken in Sanskrit. "Zeenat Aman? Parveen Babi? They're retired, man. Re-ally-tired. We could think of them for the mother's role, maybe."

I stopped making casting suggestions after that. In the end the part went to an Indian starlet from Hollywood — "she was the lead dancer in this year's Oscar ceremonies," BJ explained. (She had apparently swayed, in diaphanous veils and with a diamond in her belly button, to all the songs from *Aladdin*.)

As filming proceeded on location in Bollywood, and a dozen other scenic locales up and down the country, BJ kept insisting I come and witness the action. "We want you to play a part too," BJ insisted. "Put your signature on the film. Like Alfred Hitchcock always appeared in his movies."

"It's your movie, BJ," I said. But I couldn't help asking what walk-on part he had in mind for me. A Bollywood superstar at a film reception? A parliamentary *neta* in one of the novel's political sequences? One of the hapless directors of the hero's many films-within-the film?

"The journalist," he replied, "at the hospital, who asks the public what the dying hero means to them. Perfect part. Written for you."

Written by me, I wanted to say, but I had to admit the

idea was apt. After all, that was what I was, the writer asking what the film hero means to his audience. But I was, in the end, reluctant to put my signature on someone else's work, and I never did go to the sets.

For someone else's work is inevitably what it became. Out went my triple-narrative structure, my literary concern with reality and illusion, my attempt to use cinema as a metaphor for a larger exploration of Indian society. The film focused on the movies I'd parodied; they were, after all, what Bollywood knew, and what Bollywood did best. The larger part of my novel — the lives of my protagonists — became the smaller part of the film. Several of my favorite characters and relationships were eliminated: the bitchy gossip columnist who more or less rapes the hero, the hero's aging politician father who is bitterly disappointed in his successful son, the smarmy treasurer of the ruling party who takes advantage of the hero's lack of a moral center. The hero's discovery that a famous actress's bust is a pair of falsies proved too much even for Bollywood, and was omitted. My genderless prime minister became an imitation Indira Gandhi. Even the name of the book, *Show Business,* an allusion not only to the cinema world but also to the pretenses of politicians and the superficialities of godmen, gave way to the poster simplicity of *Bollywood.* My book had tried to do many things; by the final cut, BJ had done just one thing — he'd made a slapstick comedy about Hindi movies. "I simply left out the politics and religion," he cheerfully told *Time* magazine.

*Time* (which ran a three-page color feature paralleling BJ's *Bollywood* and Mani Ratnam's *Bombay*) clearly didn't mind. Still, the film's California premiere highlighted my ambivalence. The prominent local ethnic paper, *India West*, headlined its lengthy review "Bollywood Misses Tharoor's Insights into Film World." The critic deplored the film's "jettisoning of Tharoor's incisive look at the dream factory" and its "failure to explore the great potential of the novel." The reviewer, I noted with a pang, cited all the elements from the book that I would have liked to see in the film myself. Fortunately for BJ, hers was a minority view. The rest of the press, at festivals in Toronto and Berlin, and at premieres in California and New York, lapped it up.

And why not? Prose and cinema are different arts; they proceed from different premises, use different techniques, tell their stories in different ways. There are images that can be conveyed in a single frame that a book could not pull off in a hundred pages; equally, there are complexities on the printed page that transcend, and so escape, the images on the screen. The author is wedded to his creation, but in writing his book he is fettered only by the limits of his imagination. The film producer, on the other hand, is a craftsman who has to work within the limits of his budgets, the sets and props he finds available or affordable, the conventions of his medium, the attention span of the average cinegoer (BJ's first version, which had retained more of the book, was deemed an hour too long by the experts at Toronto), and of course the talents and abilities of his cast and crew.

And it's not as if the only results of the conversion from book to film were negative. Some shots looked exactly as I'd imagined them when I was writing; there's nothing quite like the thrill of seeing a gleam in your eye become a picture on the screen. Some film scenes actually worked better in the movie, because they came to life as they could never quite do through words alone. And I was both surprised and delighted to hear my tongue-in-cheek songs from the novel set to Tushar Parte's hummable melodies. One of the more unlikely rewards I've had from this experience is being able to revel in the improbable credits "Lyrics by Shashi Tharoor."

So when people come up to talk about "your movie," I don't disown it completely. It's dismaying, of course, that when people hear you've written a book, they treat you either with indifference or with the polite condescension one reserves for those who spend so much time doing so much work to produce so little (and for so little reward). But the moment they hear your book's been made into a movie, eyes light up, the interest they've feigned ("Oh, a book? What's it about?") becomes real ("Oh, a movie? Wow! Who's in it?"). Chunky Pandey wouldn't recognize me if he ran me over in his Mercedes, but everyone I meet at a party instantly assumes Chunky must have dropped by my place every other day to get a handle on his character. (Which, on balance, perhaps he should have.) And let's face it, films are a mass medium in a different league from books: even a flop will get seen by more people than bought the hardback. "Shashi's movie" is a phrase spoken with far more admiration than "Shashi's literary prizes." Even though, as I vainly point out, it isn't Shashi's movie.

Which means I have been getting some vicarious pleasure out of Bollywood. But the dilemma remains. Do I put up the full-size color poster BJ has given me? Display the calendar? Wear the T-shirt? Hide the book? The ultimate recourse of the author is, of course, to have it both ways. So my message to all and sundry is: If you like the film, you must read the book. But if you don't like the film, you must still read the book, to discover what the filmmaker missed.

Of course, I'm hoping Blondie doesn't read this in his bathtub.

# 32

# For Whom the Bill Tolls

D ID ANYONE NOTICE THAT JULY 21, 1999, marked the centenary of Ernest Hemingway's birth? It is curious, of
course, that a man who was seen as a such a literary giant in
his time — his suicide in 1961 even made the front page of
the Indian papers — should be so completely forgotten four
decades later. Today there seems something embarrassing
about his macho prose, the chest-out beer-swilling sentences strutting across the jungle of the page, hunting rifle
in hand, each phrase advertising the author's manhood. In
these more enlightened times, Hemingway seems as dated
as a Victorian novelist, the exemplar of another era, whose
values seem recognizable but inapplicably foreign.

And yet Ernest Hemingway had just become the exemplar of something quite contemporary, a phenomenon
very much of the last materialistic years of the twentieth
century. I have in front of me a press release from a body
calling itself Fashion Licensing of America Inc., announc-
ing good news for all those who thought Hemingway was

dead and buried (or interred in libraries). "His fame lives on," the release says, "thanks to the Ernest Hemingway Collection, a new body of licensed products embracing furniture, accessories, gifts and textiles." These feature such Hemingwayesque delights as a "Kilimanjaro king bed" for the modest sum of $3,499, an amount the grizzly writer, who prided himself on unrolling a mat by a campfire, would never have dreamed of spending on his own sleeping arrangements. If the ninety-six-piece Ernest Hemingway furniture collection (also including lamps, clocks, and even a duck decoy for the Hemingway-wannabe hunter) does not appeal, one can always pick up a $600 Mont Blanc Hemingway pen, whose cost at least can be guaranteed to inspire the short sentences for which its eponymous author was famous.

Absurd, of course, that designer accessories should be marketed in the name of a man who was famously unfussy about clothes, drink, appearance or cleanliness. "Ernest," his third wife, Martha Gellhorn, once said, "was extremely dirty, one of the most unfastidious men I've ever known." (She affectionately — and sometimes not so affectionately — called her husband "The Pig.") In Cuba he kept a pack of smelly tomcats who were allowed to march all over his furniture (but then he did not possess a $3,499 "Kilimanjaro king bed"). Though he once informed the world that Gordon's Gin had kept him alive after a plane crash — "this beverage is one of the sovereign antiseptics of our time," he wrote cheerfully; "[it] can be counted on to fortify, mollify and cauterize practically all internal or external injuries" — Hemingway was not a likely subject for the attentions of marketing men. The story is told of how a minor whisky manufacturer invited Hemingway to endorse his product, Lord Calvert whisky, by appearing in a "Men of Distinction" advertising campaign for a fee of $4,000. His retort was blunt: "I wouldn't drink the stuff for $4,000!"

So why is Ernest Hemingway now being used to sell overpriced king beds and fancy pens? The answer is simple: Hemingway the writer is no more, but Hemingway the image lives on. A larger-than-life literary giant is, in the eyes of product pitchmen, larger-after-life. People who can't be bothered to appreciate the prose but who wish to be associated with the aura of its creator can now buy into the image. Good-bye Hemingway the novelist, hello Hemingway the brand.

What are the chances that this American trend might also, as so often happens in our globalized world, make its way into our country? Indian writers are lately beginning to receive almost as much attention as their Western counterparts. Even if literary product licensing is still an unknown art in India, it is surely not too early to consider the possibilities of paying commercial homage to our literary venerables. A Mulk Raj Anand coolie badge, for instance, might be just the thing to accessorize the latest Bina Ramani blouse. Or perhaps the Cottage Industries Emporium might honor Kamala Markandeya by actually selling nectar in a sieve? Equally up their street could be the Raja Rao serpent and rope set, in leather and coir, perhaps, or an Anita Desai crying peacock, tastefully done in brass. The possibilities are limitless: *ganga-jal* in a U-shaped urn could be sold as the Manohar Malgaonkar Bend in the Ganges, and any number of post-Kargil mementoes could be recycled as Bhabani

Bhattacharya's Shadows from Ladakh. More practical shoppers could take home Raj Kamal Jha's slightly soiled Blue Bedspread. For the better-heeled buyer with a taste for objets d'art, a fragment of rubble and a bulb could constitute an Attia Hosain Sunlight on a Broken Column. And I haven't even begun to mention the potential of an entire Malgudi Collection honoring R. K. Narayan's fictional small town (a slightly sagging string charpoy could, for instance, rival the attractions of Hemingway's Kilimanjaro king bed).

But something tells me India is not quite ready for all this yet. The director of Kerala tourism told me how he had made plans for an Arundhati Roy tour of the Vembanad backwaters, to rake dollars off the foreign tourists clamoring for a glimpse of Ayemenem and associated locales in *The God of Small Things*. The idea was brilliant, but it was promptly vetoed by the state government as unseemly. Writers have their place in literate India, it seems, but only on the bookshelves. Hemingway, now spinning in his grave, would no doubt have approved.

# 33

# The Rise of the Political Litterateur

DURING A 1989 VISIT TO INDIA in the aftermath of the publication of *The Great Indian Novel,* someone who claimed to be a regular reader of one of my columns (always a dangerous species, the regular reader) offered me a challenge: to reconcile, in my next column, my interests in literature and international affairs. I told him it couldn't be done, except in jest — imagining which works of literature would be most appropriate for which then-prevalent international situation (*The Winter of Our Discontent* for Romania that year, perhaps, though *The Grapes of Wrath* would do just as well; *One Hundred Years of Solitude* for Albania's isolationist Politburo; *Joy in the Morning* for the release of Nelson Mandela, and so on.) He seemed to accept the answer, but my conscience wasn't so obliging. Regular readers, it inconveniently insisted, must be obliged.

Then the elevation of Václav Havel to the presidency of Czechoslovakia gave me a better answer. For here was the perfect marriage of the worlds of literature and international affairs — a playwright ascending to political power. Havel, a longtime dissident who had spent many years imprisoned and silenced by his own government because they feared his words, had become a symbol and a spokesman for the forces of democratic reform in his country. Words, he once declared, "have the power to change history." By his own triumphal ascent to power he demonstrated that the writer of words can also change history, indeed can make as well as reflect it.

Not every writer becomes, or even tries to become, a president, but half a world away in Peru, Mario Vargas Llosa, the eminent novelist, tried and failed, after handily leading in the public opinion polls, for the same post in his country. Vargas Llosa had not suffered the physical incarceration that Havel endured, but he became impatient with the mere function of observing and writing about the problems of his nation. As an author, he felt, he "had a unique understanding of the people, their needs, their concerns, their spirit." He therefore entered the fray at what most analysts considered a desperate time for Peru, a country racked by hyperinflation, drugs, social problems, and the crippling terrorism of the Sendoro Luminoso or Shining Path movement. Perhaps to the surprise only of non-Latin Americans, he was promptly adopted by a conservative party as its official candidate. Though he lost, his profession was not discredited; a notch lower in the pecking order, Nicaraguan novelist Sergio Ramirez sought reelection the same month as his country's vice president.

The closest equivalent in India might be the electoral success of Tamil Nadu chief minister M. Karunanidhi, though as a screenwriter his words reach the public only indirectly, through the lips of actors. Former prime minister P. V. Narasimha Rao is a rare example of a politician who became a novelist; his *Insider* was too thinly veiled an account of his own career to qualify convincingly as fiction. If true novelists, playwrights, and poets have been less successful in influencing India's political destiny, journalists have demonstrated the power of words to shake governments (and indeed, as the victories of several journalists seeking seats in Parliament suggests, to win votes for themselves).

Some, of course, may argue that journalism is hardly literature, even if sometimes it has been indistinguishable from fiction. And at least the Indian journalist, like the Indian litterateur, is free to write what he wishes to. The greatest challenge for writers is when they have to function in societies that do not grant them this freedom. Then the function of literature becomes more than the creative rendering of social observations. In societies where truth is what the government says is true, literature must depict a deeper truth that the culture needs to grasp in order to survive. Kurt Vonnegut once compared the writer to the canary sent down a mine shaft to determine whether there is enough air for the miners to work: if the canary suffocates or comes up gasping for air, the miners know something has to be done. In many countries, it is the writers' gasping cries at their own suffocation that has brought about the most fundamental changes. As the Nobel Prize–winning Italian novelist Italo Calvino put it, "The paradox of the power of literature [is] that only when it is persecuted does it show its true powers." President Havel expressed it with even greater intensity. "I inhabit a system," he said, "in which words are capable of shaking the entire structure of government, where words can prove mightier than ten military divisions. . . . The word Solidarity was capable of shaking an entire power bloc."

It is probably no accident, therefore, that some of the world's greatest literature in recent years has been produced by writers who are either in exile from oppressive political systems (Gabriel García Márquez, Milan Kundera, Breyten Breytenbach, Aleksandr Solzhenitsyn) or struggling to hold up a mirror to the oppressive structures within which they live (André Brink and Nadine Gordimer in South Africa, Pablo Neruda in Chile, Boris Pasternak in the Soviet Union, Solzhenitsyn before his exile, Havel himself). Literature has always had the potential to raise the awkward question, to probe the deeper reality, to awaken the dormant consciousness, and therefore to subvert the established order. Which may explain why good writers rarely have the opportunity to make effective presidents. They are better at revealing than at ruling.

# 34

# Homage in Huesca

"WHY HUESCA?" our friends asked when my former wife and I told them where we wanted to go. It was 1980, and we were on our first visit to Spain, then newly emerged into democracy after four decades of Franco's fascism. But Huesca was no tourist spot: it was an obscure town on the way to nowhere. To get there, we would have to risk country roads of unpredictable quality. And then our homeward ascent through the Pyrenees, we were warned, would be unnecessarily arduous. "Forget it," our friends said.

We couldn't. There was something we had to do in Huesca.

So we wound our way tortuously through the rugged hills of the Sierra de la Peña, till the road flattened out across deserted scrubland and a weather-beaten sign told us we had reached our destination.

Huesca was as nondescript a provincial town as our friends had said it would be. But we had a specific objective in mind. Not the cathedral, to which our Michelin guidebook accorded one star. Not even the traditional bustling market-place, which Hemingway might have immortalized in a couple of paragraphs. What we wanted, as we'd explained to our disbelieving friends, was something altogether simpler.

We had come to Huesca for a cup of coffee.

My wife scanned the storefronts as I turned in to unfa-miliar streets. Twice I nearly stopped the car, but Minu's sense of occasion was not satisfied. "No, not here," she said. "It's not quite right." I drove on.

It was springtime, as it had been decades earlier, in 1937, when Huesca had acquired its brief spasm of importance as a military stronghold of Franco's army in the Spanish Civil War. The ragtag Republican forces, resisting him in their forlorn fight against fascism, had encircled the town. Their ranks included a motley collection of international volun-teers — idealists and opportunists, anarchists, Communists, and passionate democrats. Among them was a gaunt, con-sumptive English writer who called himself George Orwell.

The Republicans, poorly armed, badly led, hopelessly organized, and racked by treachery and dissension, be-sieged Huesca for months. Amid the blood and grime of the grueling campaign, the inspiriting word was passed through the frontlines: "Tomorrow we'll have coffee in Huesca."

Orwell took heart from the prospect. "Tomorrow we'll have coffee in Huesca": it was the kind of false promise that sustains morale in every war, like "We'll be home for Christ-mas." The siege of Huesca dragged on, and the slogan's op-timism rang increasingly hollow. Attrition took its toll on lives, strategic objectives, hope. Huesca, impregnable in fascist hands, seemed to represent the utter futility of the cause of freedom.

George Orwell, destined to become one of the world's great voices of freedom, was wounded in action on the outskirts of Huesca. He left for home on a stretcher, bitter in his disappointment. "If I ever go back to Spain," he wrote in his searing *Homage to Catalonia*, "I shall make a point of having a cup of coffee in Huesca."

But Huesca did not fall. Franco and fascism triumphed in Spain, and Orwell never saw Huesca again.

"Here," Minu said abruptly. "This is it. Stop the car."

We were at a modest little café, as unremarkable as the ones she had earlier rejected. But across the road, its sign bright in the sun, stood an imposing building. For forty years under the Franco regime, the long arm of the law had ended in a clenched fist — that of the dreaded Guardia Civil. Minu had stopped me in front of its local headquarters.

"What will you have, señor, señora?" the waiter asked us as we sat down. "Lunch? Dessert?"

I looked over his shoulder, across the road, at two civil guards in the uniform of their newly restored democracy. They stood stiffly at attention, rifles in hand, guarding the gates of their establishment.

"No, thanks," I replied at last. "All we need is a cup of coffee."

# 35

# Is There a "St. Stephen's School of Literature"?

A FEW YEARS AGO I received an interesting paper from a professor at my old college, St. Stephen's, an elegant oasis of red brick on the bustling outskirts of Delhi. The professor, Aditya Bhattacharjea, was an economist, but despite this disqualification his paper intrigued me. Remarking that a majority of the country's leading English-language writers — he named Rukun Advani, Upamanyu Chatterjee, Amitav Ghosh, Mukul Kesavan, Anurag Mathur, Allan Sealy, and myself — were all roughly contemporaries at St. Stephen's, Professor Bhattacharjea posited the existence of a new literary phenomenon, a "St. Stephen's School of Literature."

The case was cogently argued in a thoughtful and elegant essay. Scholars like Ranga Rao, himself a novelist, and Harish Trivedi had called the rise to prominence of these Stephanian writers "the single most significant development of Indian writing in English of the 1980s." Trivedi described them, in a paraphrase of Macaulay, as "Stephanians in taste, in opinions, in morals and in intellect." Others had been more cutting, but equally validated the label: Alok Rai, for instance, wrote of "the recent outbreak of bright, clever Indian writing in English. . . . 'St. Stephen's' is code for writing which is reminiscent of privileged, bustling quads and redolent of jockstraps and cynical, brilliant undergraduates hyped up by their gonads and their wit." Aditya Bhattacharjea concluded from these and other literary references that "a new phenomenon bearing the name of the College has indeed been identified on the Indian literary scene."

The notion of a St. Stephen's School of Literature was itself, of course, a wonderfully Stephanian idea, and as an Old Boy I was both amused and bemused. Amused, because the idea was, for any Stephanian writer, a diverting one to contemplate; bemused, because the assumptions underlying the notion of such a school were problematic enough without the additional burden of being described as its exemplar ("Shashi Tharoor, possibly the most 'Stephanian' of the novelists," Bhattacharjea wrote in his essay.)

Since I did not study English at college and therefore possess neither a theoretical grounding in literature nor a critical vocabulary to articulate my prejudices, my reactions to this thesis are not as scholarly as its proponents'. It strikes me, though, that the existence of a school should imply something more than the mere fact that a number of writers share the same alma mater (as the college's notorious student paper *Kooler Talk* might have put it, the "school" must mean more than the college). If there is a St. Stephen's School of Literature (and if there is, let us call it SSSL henceforth, in homage to the Stephanian addiction to acronyms), its members must have similarities in their literary outputs — similarities of style, theme, content, sensibility, or some combination of these — that both link them and set them apart from other, non-Stephanian writers. There must also be some continuing affinity among the members, some literary bond that reinforces the exclusivity of their mutual club. As I will explain, I am not sure that these two requirements can be found among the eligible members of the putative SSSL.

But first, what does the very name St. Stephen's stand for to the outsiders whose comments have sparked this debate? To non-Stephanians, St. Stephen's in this context largely conjures up three overlapping concepts, none of which is meant to be flattering — elitism, Anglophilia, and deracination. Before one can discuss a Stephanian school, one is obliged to confront this stereotype head-on.

Whether or not there is an SSSL, there is certainly a spirit that can be called Stephanian: after all, I spent three years living in and celebrating it. Stephania was both an ethos and a condition to which we aspired. Elitism was part of it, but by no means the whole. In any case "Mission College" elitism had a self-fulfilling quality about it that made it the best guarantee of its own perpetuation. St. Stephen's attracts such a high caliber of student that it is virtually assured of excellent examination results irrespective of the competence of the faculty. Further, its alumni either originate in, or graduate to, such a privileged and influential stratum of society that they constitute a network in government, in business, in the media, on which every Stephanian can seek to draw.

But this is still elitism in an Indian context, albeit one shaped, like so many Indian institutions, by a colonial legacy. There is no denying that the aim of the Cambridge Brotherhood in founding St. Stephen's in 1881 was to produce more obedient subjects to serve Her Britannic Majesty; their idea of constructive missionary activity was to bring the intellectual and social atmosphere of Camside to the dry dustplains of Delhi. Improbably enough, they succeeded, and the resultant hybrid outlasted the Raj. St. Stephen's in the early 1970s was an institution whose students sustained a Shakespeare Society and a Criterion Club, organized union debates on such statements as "In the opinion of this House the opinion of this House does not matter," staged plays and wrote poetry, ran India's only faculty-sanctioned Practical Joke Competition (in memory of P. G. Wodehouse's irrepressible Lord Ickenham), invented the "Winter Festival" of collegiate cultural competition, which was imitated at universities across the country, invariably reached the annual intercollege cricket final (and turned up in large numbers to cheer the Stephanian cricketers on to their accustomed victory), maintained a careful distinction between the Junior Common Room and the Senior Combination Room, and allowed the world's only non-Cantabridgian "gyps" to serve their meals and make their beds. And if the punts never came to the Jamuna, the puns flowed on the pages of *Kooler Talk* and the cyclostyled *Spice* (the underground rag put out by the Wodehouse Society, whose typing mistakes were deliberate, and deliberately hilarious).

This was the St. Stephen's I knew, and none of us who lived and breathed the Stephanian air saw any alien affectation in it. For one thing, St. Stephen's also embraced the Hindi movies at nearby suburbs and trips to the aluminum-shed "dhaba" at the corner of the campus, where individual cigarettes were sold to impecunious students; the nocturnal Informal Discussion Group saw articulate discussion of political issues, and the Social Service League actually went out and performed social service; and even for the "pseuds," the height of career aspiration was the Indian Administrative Service, not a multinational corporation. The Stephanian could hardly be deracinated and still manage to bloom. It was against Indian targets that the Stephanian set his goals, and by Indian assumptions that he sought to attain them. (A self-protective disclaimer to feminists about my pronouns: I studied at St. Stephen's before its co-edification in 1975.)

At the same time St. Stephen's was, astonishingly for a college in Delhi, insulated to a remarkable extent from the prejudices of middle-class Indian life. It mattered little where you were from, which Indian language you spoke at home, what version of religious faith you espoused. When I joined the college in 1972 from Calcutta, the son of a southern newspaper executive, I did not have to worry about fitting in: we were all minorities at St. Stephen's, and all part of one eclectic polychrome culture. Five of the preceding ten union presidents had been non-Delhiite non-Hindus (four Muslims and a Christian), and they had all been fairly elected against candidates from the "majority" community. But at St. Stephen's religion and region were not the distinctions that mattered: what counted was whether you were "in residence" or a "dayski" (day-scholar), a "science type" or a "DramSoc type," a sportsman or a univ "topper" (or best of all, both). Caste and creed were no bar, but these other categories determined your share of the Stephanian experience.

This blurring of conventional distinctions was a crucial element of Stephania. "Sparing" (a Stephanianism derived from "spare time") with the more congenial of your comrades in residence — though it could leave you with a near-fatal faith in coffee, conversation, and crosswords as ends in themselves — was manifestly more important than attending classes. (And in any case, you learned as much from approachable faculty members outside the classroom as inside it.) Being hazed ("ragged," in our argot) outside the back gate of the women's college Miranda House, having a late coffee in your block tutor's room, hearing outrageous (and largely apocryphal) tales about recent Stephanians who were no longer around to contradict them, seeing your name punned with in *Kooler Talk*, were all integral parts of the Stephanian culture, and of the ways in which this culture was transmitted to each successive batch of Stephanians.

Three years is, of course, a small — and decreasing — proportion of my life, but my three years at St. Stephen's marked me for all the years to follow. Partly this was because I joined the college a few months after my sixteenth birthday and left it a few months after my nineteenth, so that I was at St. Stephen's at an age when any experience would have had a lasting effect. But equally vital was the institution itself, its atmosphere and history, its student body and teaching staff, its sense of itself and how that sense was communicated to each individual character in the Stephanian story. Too many Indian colleges are places for lectures, rote learning, memorizing, regurgitation; St. Stephen's encouraged random reading, individual note-taking, personal tutorials, extracurricular development. Elsewhere you learned to answer the questions; at college, you learned to question the answers. Some of us went further, and questioned the questions.

So, to return to the possible existence of a St. Stephen's school of Indo-Anglian writing: I have to admit that St. Stephen's influenced me fundamentally, gave me my basic faith in all-inclusive, multanimous, free-thinking cultures, helped shape my mind and define my sense of myself in relation to the world, and so, inevitably, influenced what I have done later in life — as a man, as a United Nations official, and as a writer. Stephania encouraged the development of qualities that would stand writers in good stead. But I had been writing well before I came to St. Stephen's — my first story was published more than five years before I entered college — and I did not cease to learn when I left St. Stephen's, so I cannot say that (except for the few short stories I wrote in college and about college) either the style or the content of my writing is primarily or exclusively Stephanian. And while my Stephanian friendships are important to me, and my association with the college is something of which I am inordinately proud, neither relates much to matters literary. Indeed, practically none of the other early-1970s Stephanian writers who have since distinguished themselves did any writing while I knew them at St. Stephen's. (I remember Amitav Ghosh as a diligent reporter for All-India Radio's "Roving Microphone," and Allan Sealy's prowess with the guitar was the stuff of legend, but only Anurag Mathur, apart from myself, published fiction while he was at St. Stephen's.) To trace retrospective connections in a common "school" would, if I remember my subsidiary classes in philosophy right, be guilty of the logical fallacy of *post hoc, ergo propter hoc*. It might have been different if those who sharpened their own, and each other's, linguistic rapiers at *Kooler Talk* or *Spice* had all gone on to churn out comparable novels; but the campus journalists of my time have all firmly resisted the temptation to produce literary fiction.

Those who have seen a distinctively "Stephanian" quality in some Indo-Anglian writers seem to use the term (largely, I might add, with pejorative intent) to include notions of elitism, privilege, irreverence, flippant wit, cleverness in the use of language, and deracination from the Indian mainstream, wherever that may flow. They do not appear to include the secularism, the pan-Indian outlook, the well-rounded education, the eclectic social interests, the questioning spirit, and the meritocratic culture that are equally vital ingredients of the Stephanian ethos. To the extent that all these elements characterize the work of Stephanian writers, one might be able to talk of a Stephanian school of literature; but the truth is that these qualities, positive as well as negative, are not all found in all the Stephanian novelists, whose works quite naturally manifest as many divergences as similarities. And many of the presumed elements of an SSSL can be spotted in other Indian writers of the same generation who have not come within sniffing distance of St. Stephen's College; Vikram Chandra, Richard Crasta, and Sunetra Gupta are just three of the names that come to mind. What is being described as "Stephanian" writing is in fact characteristic of an entire generation of Indian writers in English, who grew up without the shadow of the Englishman judging their prose, who used it unselfconsciously in their daily lives in independent India, and who eventually wrote fiction in it as naturally as they would have written their university exams, their letters home, or the notes they slipped to each other in their classrooms.

I would argue, in other words, that whatever the Stephanian writers have in common, they also share with non-Stephanian Indian writers in English (indeed, it is ironic to see Stephanian writing being criticized for showy prose and brittle wit by non-Stephanian reviewers using language that reveals the same qualities.) And what they do not have in common (the gulf between the concerns and aspirations of any two of the writers to whom St. Stephen's can lay claim) is sufficiently significant to dilute any thought of an SSSL.

This is also borne out by the absence of what I have earlier called a continuing affinity, a sort of literary bond of loyalty, amongst the members of any SSSL. St. Stephen's is after all a college, and like all colleges it breeds its share of resentments; the Stephanian writer thus brings a great deal of nonliterary baggage to his encounters with Stephanian critics. Of the more than a hundred and forty reviews *The Great Indian Novel* received on five continents, only three were largely negative; two of those — and I make the point a little ruefully — were by contemporaries of mine at St. Stephen's.

So there may not be a St. Stephen's School of Literature, but what its supposed adherents have been writing deserves a place in the national literary canon. I have often argued that criticisms of Indian writing in English are often based on a notion of authenticity that is highly contestable. The pun-dropping Stephanian is as Indian as the Punjabi peasant of the Pune professor; and if what he writes is not sufficiently rooted in the earth of the Gangetic plains to pass muster with the self-appointed guardians of Indianness, it has its place within a realm of experience that is still uniquely Indian. The frame of reference of the Stephanian novelist may not be that of R. K. Narayan, but then Narayan's was not exactly that of, say, Thakazhi Sivasankara Pillai — and India is large enough to embrace all three as her own.

The critic Harish Trivedi has asserted that Stephanian writers are "cut off from the experiential mainstream, and from [India's] common cultural matrix." India is too diverse for any single "experiential mainstream" to be easily identi-fied, but the charge of being outside the culture is a more serious one. R. K. Narayan once wrote of an English-medium school called St. Stephen's whose students are obliged to first rub off the sandal-paste caste-marks from the forehead before they enter its portals; Trivedi approvingly sees this as a metaphor of Stephanian deracination, with "St. Stephen's" a synonym "for those who have erased their antecedents." I see no particular shame in the erasure of casteism from the classroom. But the more important point is that Stephanian writers do share a "common cultural matrix" with other Indians, though not one smeared with sandal-paste caste-marks. It is a "cultural matrix" that consists of an urban upbringing and a pan-national outlook on the Indian reality, expressed in English but drawing sustenance from nonanglophone Indian sources — languages, films, music, food, clothing — that Stephanians share with other Indians.

Of course the attention being paid to Stephanians should not be at the expense of the very worthwhile writing being done by non-Stephanians of every stripe, particularly in other Indian languages, which deserve to be better translated in order to command the national audience that English gives the Indo-Anglians. But India is a big country: it has room for many schools of literature, and for many colleges — and cottages, and garrets — to produce them.

# 36

# Quotes of Many Colors

IT WAS MY MOTHER, her keen eye diligently scanning the press for items of interest, who spotted the ad in the newspaper. "Now," it said, "you can quote Kalidasa and not just Shakespeare; Amartya Sen and not just Adam Smith . . . Tagore and Tharoor." That, of course, was the clincher. (Show me a writer without an ego, and I'll show you a very good actor.) When she sent me the clipping, my first reaction was to give thanks that someone had finally done it — produced, to cite the ad again, "for the very first time, a fully cross-indexed Indian source for Indian quotations." My second reaction was to fear that, in the face of so gigantic (and unprecedented) a task, it might not have been done well. And my third was to immediately ask a friend traveling to Delhi to pick me up a copy of the book, the *Enquire Dictionary of Quotations.*

It wasn't, my friend tells me, widely available; she tried half a dozen bookshops, some rather prestigious, before finding one that stocked it. (They all had the *Penguin Dictionary of Quotations* instead, which features no Indian author.) But it came at last, a handsomely bound volume of 244 pages with a striking yellow-and-black cover. In an introductory note the editor, T. J. S. George, observes that "the *Oxford Dictionary of Quotations* has thirty-eight pages of quotations from the Bible, not one from the Bhagavad Gita." Referring to the dominance of Western source material in India, he asks, "Is it any wonder that Shakespeare is a household name in Sholapur and Thirunelveli while Kalidasa is not?"

The challenge the compiler has set for himself is undoubtedly a laudable one — to bring within the reach of the Indian reader in English quotations from Indian classics as well as contemporary writers that deserve the familiarity that well-worn Western words enjoy. Every reader and writer has indulged in the habit of looking up a familiar quotation; indeed, many of us have jotted down memorable quotes over the years ourselves, seeking inspiration or even just reminders of mind-opening thoughts or startling words. To read lines from the Rig Veda, the Upanishads, and the surviving works of Kalidasa, neatly arranged and sourced, is to rejoice in the thrill of discovery. To reread the words and the wisdom of a Nehru or a Tagore is to marvel again at the intellectual giants who brought us that freedom of mind and spirit that is just as important as the political freedom for which they strived. There is no question that the *Enquire Dictionary of Quotations* will offer any questing Indian many hours of rewarding browsing.

But as with most first attempts, the editor has, alas, made curious choices of both commission and omission that detract from the value of his effort. The book's arrangement is a complete shambles. It idiosyncratically sets out to be chronological rather than alphabetical: I have seen books of quotations arranged by name and others arranged by subject, but why on earth privilege the date of birth of the author over any other attribute of his material? This is complicated enough for a reader wanting to quickly look up a particular writer, but then, three-quarters of the way through the book, the chronology collapses, so that V. B. Karnik, born 1916, appears after Uma Maheshwari, born 1974 (and in some cases no date of birth is listed at all). Worse, this is a book of Indian quotations: what on earth is that wonderful Palestinian, Edward Said, doing in it? Or Bertrand Russell, with an unmemorable line about Nehru? If the (unannounced) intention is also to include great quotations about India, the list is woefully sparse; Churchill appears with a tossed-off comment about Indians being a "beastly people with a beastly religion," but none of his more considered utterances on the country is included. Worse, his well-known crack about Mahatma Gandhi being a "half-naked fakir" appears under the "Gandhi" entry, not under "Churchill." Only British quotations on Gandhi feature, so Einstein and Romain Rolland are absent. There is only one quote about Tagore (Yeats's famous comment that "no Indian knows English"), whereas one might have included a dozen others, or left them all out. The editor clearly could not make up his mind about how far he should go to include foreigners saying pithy things about India; by including just a handful of comments, he denies himself the excuse that he only wished to include Indian sources, while laying himself open to the charge that his omissions are so extensive that they undermine his choices.

That is also a charge that applies to many of the selections of Indian quotations. Tagore devotees will miss several of their favorites; his immortal "When I go from hence, let this be my parting word," the poem found written out in Wilfred Owen's diary the day before the great British poet was killed in World War I, is one example of an unforgivable omission. Nehru is superbly represented, Ram Manohar Lohia impressively so, Gandhiji poorly (no examples of his puckish wit, for instance, are included) and Atal Bihari Vajpayee, after a lifetime in politics, parliament, and poetry, gets just one line. Modern Indian poets in general receive a good airing, none better than the great late A. K. Ramanaujan, but Gieve Patel's classic "On Being Neither Hindu nor Muslim in India" is absent. (And as for Shashi Tharoor, the compiler has found just four quotes, all from *The Great Indian Novel*, whereas had he only asked, I might have directed him to a dozen more that have been widely cited!) This is not to belittle the awesome task before the compiler and his helpers; but while for those who have passed away, the editor must rely on his own extensive reading, he might have done well to solicit material from living authors to give himself a better range to choose from.

Finally, the indexing is sometimes a mystery. Having organized the book neither by subject nor author, the editor has sensibly included both a subject index and an author index. Alas, the latter is whimsical (Charan Singh appears under *C*, for instance, Romila Thapar under *R*, and O. V.

Vijayan under *O!*), and the former is erratic. Kalidasa's lovely lines about the monsoon — "a source of fascination to amorous women, the constant friend to trees, shrubs and creepers, the very life and breath of all living beings, this season of rains" — can be found neither under "season," nor "rains": how will a student be able to quote Kalidasa on the subject of rainy weather by recourse to this index?

"Readers may agree," Mr. George forewarns us, "that an imperfect collection is better than no collection." Absolutely; but after offering congratulations for this imperfect job, may this reader urge Mr. George to lose no time preparing an improved second edition of what could be, but is not yet, an indispensable reference source for all thinking Indians?

# 37

# The Pornography of Poverty?

CALCUTTA, NO STRANGER TO CULTURAL CONTROVERSY — its citizens once rioted and burned trams to protest a Paris writer's expulsion from the Cinémathèque Française — again hit the literary headlines in 1990. This time, it was the filming of *City of Joy*, based on Dominique Lapierre's 1986 bestseller about poverty and piety in this Bengali city, that pitted outraged Calcuttans against the movie's bewildered, and largely American, crew.

Director Roland Joffe was quoted as saying he had an easier time making *The Killing Fields* on the Cambodian border and *The Mission* in the jungles of Colombia. His film has been the subject of a variety of forms of vocal protest, ranging from editorials and lawsuits to demonstrations and (in one episode) bombs being thrown on the set. A Bengali reporter covering the picketing died after allegedly being beaten up by two of Joffe's assistants. The courts kept the crew's cameras idle for weeks, before allowing restricted public filming on holidays.

On the face of it, *City of Joy*'s troubles seemed to confirm India's reputation for thin-skinned hypocrisy. The protestors were angry about the film's focus on the city's despair
and degradation; the filmmakers pointed out, not unreason-
ably, that these do exist. Calcuttans dreaded yet another
depiction of poverty, prostitution, and urban squalor un-
leavened by any acknowledgment that their city has for
over two centuries been India's cultural capital, a metropo-
lis of art galleries, avant-garde theaters, and overflowing
bookshops, whose coffeehouse waiters speak knowledge-
ably of Godard and Truffaut. The filmmakers responded
that that may well be true, but that's not what their film is
about: it's about poverty and suffering and death — all of
which can be found in good measure in Calcutta's slums —
and about the resilience of the human spirit in the face of
tragedy. They saw their work as a tribute to Calcutta, a city
of misery that is nonetheless a city of joy. Those who want
them to turn their cameras on the other Calcutta, Joffe says,
are only trying to camouflage the painful reality.

Perhaps — but whose reality? Lapierre's book was
burned by those he wrote about, the residents of the slum of
Pilkhana. Even those who did not condone the violence and
extremism of some of the protestors sympathized with their
objections. The way they told it, the book was bad enough;
with the film, Calcutta would become the favorite pinup of
the pornographers of poverty. Westerners were going to
munch popcorn in air-conditioned theaters as they stared at
flickering images of dying Indian babies. This is a new kind
of voyeurism, which has no interest in the totality of the
Calcuttan reality, only in that part of it that titillates the

Western conscience. And don't forget the racism: in the book and in the film, the Indians are poor wretches who need cinegenic whites to give them succor. Calcutta doesn't matter for itself; it is merely the backdrop for the beatification of a Polish priest and the self-realization of an American doctor (played by *Dirty Dancing*'s Patrick Swayze).

The more thoughtful of the protestors say they would have no problem with a different film on the same subject. They are proud of Indian directors, like Satyajit Ray, Ritwik Ghatak, and Mrinal Sen, who have made vivid and convincing films on Bengali poverty. Neither Lapierre nor Joffe, they argue, feel the same empathy. Worse, by focusing on Western protagonists, they implicitly deny the dedication and sacrifice of thousands of Calcuttans — rich, poor, and middle-class — who have devoted their time and their resources to helping their fellow citizens. Even Mother Teresa couldn't have achieved a fraction of what she did without her overwhelmingly Indian legions of volunteers and nuns, none of whom happen to look like Patrick Swayze. Indians are struggling with dignity and selflessness to overcome their own problems. The book, and the film, does them a disservice.

It is a persuasive case, passionately argued by Calcuttan intellectuals. And yet I found myself deeply ambivalent about it. As an Indian, I don't particularly relish what Lapierre did in his book; I am reminded of Mahatma Gandhi, sixty years earlier, calling the American traveler Katharine Mayo's *Mother India* "a drain-inspector's report." As a writer, though, I was troubled by my Calcuttan friends' implicit condonation of censorship; they seemed to be saying to Lapierre and Joffe, This is our poverty, you can't depict it. I cannot accept that, any more than I can accept the suggestion that Peter Brook had no right to make his version of our epic, the Mahabharata.

I cannot accept the notion that the suffering of the Third World's underclass is not a fit subject for First World filmmakers. On the contrary, I spent more than a decade as a UN refugee official trying to get the media of the haves interested in the problems of the have-nots. I am aware that, in aiming at a Western audience, Joffe had to frame his story from the perspective of the outsiders, just as Candice Bergen as the photographer Margaret Bourke-White got more footage in the film *Gandhi* than a dozen Indian figures with a greater claim to a share in the Mahatma's life. Before seeing the film, I feared that the Indian poor would be the objects of Mr. Joffe's lens, rather than its subjects; *City of Joy* would be less their story than Patrick Swayze's. Like the Calcutta protestors, I resented that, but unlike them, it is a price I was willing to pay. (As it happens, the finished film ennobled and empowered its main Indian character, powerfully portrayed by the great Indian actor Om Puri.)

But I was willing to risk a bad, even exploitative, film in defense of the principle that Joffe has as much right to make a film about India as I have to set my next novel in America. And — just as Candice Bergen's presence helped get Gandhi's message to a vast new audience — I know that Joffe's film can do far more to make the West's rich aware of the East's poor than the more authentic films of Third

World directors, which won't garner any Academy Awards or reach a fraction of the audience that *City of Joy* will.

Those are two good reasons why, when I went to Calcutta during the filming, I refused to join my friends on the picket line.

# V

## Interrogations

# 38

# Bookless in Baghdad

I TRAVELED TO BAGHDAD IN MID-FEBRUARY 1998 not as an Indian writer but in the course of my "other life" as a United Nations official. The world was largely focused on two dramas at the time, both involving issues of "internal affairs" and "access to presidential sites" — the crisis over United Nations weapons inspections in Iraq, and the Monica Lewinsky scandal in Washington. It was the former that took me, at very short notice, to Baghdad with an "advance team" to prepare the sudden visit of the secretary-general of the United Nations. The necessary groundwork laid, there was just enough time to catch a few glimpses of the Iraqi capital, away from UN business, before the political negotiations began.

Where does a non-Arabic speaker go in quest of literary pleasures in Baghdad? The answer, I was told by a senior UN colleague resident there, was to what visitors call the "book souk." This is actually a longish street, Al Mutanabi, rather than, as the word "souk" implies, an enclosed bazaar.

Appropriately enough, the street is named for a legendary tenth-century poet, Tayyeb Mutanabi, author of the immortal lines I would later come across cited by the *Washington Post*'s Nora Boustany: "Not everything a man longs for is within his reach / For gusts of wind can blow against a ship's desires."

The booksellers of Al Mutanabi were for the most part people whose desires had been buffeted by strong gusts of wind from abroad — international sanctions that had paralyzed their country's normal trade and sent their economy and currency into free fall. On both sides of Al Mutanabi, old (and some new) publications were laid out for sale on the sidewalks; magazines and volumes were arrayed on sheets, racks, and cartons the length of the street, from a busy intersection at one end to a cul-de-sac at the other. This was not, for an Indian visitor, extraordinary in itself, reminiscent as it was of the pavement bookstores of Calcutta's College Street. But what was different was the added pathos that many of the books and journals on sale were from the personal libraries of families devastated by life under sanctions, who now had to sell their volumes to survive.

And what a cornucopia was laid out for the indiscriminate reader! Books and periodicals overflowed the dusty sidewalks. Some were leather-bound, some tattered; first editions of rare books rubbed spines with dusty paperbacks from forgotten best-seller lists; technical textbooks sat alongside primly covered Arabic girlie magazines from a more modest era. The volumes were mainly in Arabic, but the makeshift stalls also featured a multiplicity of foreign publications, especially in English (though German, French, and — according to a Scandinavian colleague — even Swedish popped up too). Here I spotted a lovingly thumbed reference book, there a brittle 1950s set of *Time* magazines; 1970s Lebanese reprints of nineteenth-century British classics sat side by side with out-of-date almanacs and even, bizarrely, an old telephone directory. Many of the English titles seemed incongruous on an Arab street — a paperback of Leon Uris's *Exodus*, for instance, or even more startling, Grace Metalious's *Peyton Place*. Though Iraq had long enjoyed a reputation as among the most secular and cosmopolitan of Arab societies, adversity had noticeably begun to breed piety: many of the newer volumes were Korans, some handsomely bound, and they were selling more briskly than the pulp fiction — or the men's magazines.

I had heard from foreigners of the bargains to be had at the book souk: stories, perhaps apocryphal, were told at the UN cafeteria of opportunist colleagues like the one who had picked up a first edition of T. E. Lawrence's *Seven Pillars of Wisdom* for the equivalent of seven cents in Iraq's dramatically depreciated currency (at a penny a pillar, the buyer clearly had acquired his wisdom on the cheap). What I had not heard about, however, was the avid interest of the local population in the offerings of the book souk. Even at an early hour on a weekend (I was there on a Friday, the Islamic Sunday), there was a crowd of Iraqis on the pavement, browsing, chatting, laying out more books in remarkably orderly fashion, eager to share their wares with a visitor. Iraqis are a famously literate people; an old saw about the Middle East has it that "the Egyptians write, the Lebanese publish, and the Iraqis read." Here was proof of this, in these often-perused, carefully preserved books bought decades ago, many with ownership proudly inscribed on the flyleaf, some lovingly annotated in the margins. It was easy to imagine them on the shelves of middle-class living rooms in educated homes, now brought out by their owners to help fill stomachs where they had only, in the past, salved souls.

The threat of bombs had been in the air for weeks, and Baghdad was full of journalists looking for news that would be obsolete in minutes. But here in the souk of Al Mutanabi there was a sense that there is a world beyond the immediate, that the wisdom of antiquity could prevail over the news flash of the moment, that poetry could still trump poverty, that books might buffer you from bombs. Amid the lingering remnants of remembered reading from an age when leisure was a choice rather than an imposition, the avid Iraqi buyers appeared to affirm a life beyond the headlines, a life sustained by the timeless pleasure that the printed page — read, reread, passed on from hand to hand — would continue to provide.

"I forgive time its sins," Tayyeb Mutanabi had written, "if it maintains friendships and safeguards books." The reverence for reading resonates in his thousand-year-old dictum: "A home without a library is an arid desert." Each book for sale on that sidewalk souk named for him seemed to me to be one more paving stone in a journey that was transforming home after Iraqi home into a trackless desert.

Perhaps I was being unduly romantic. On my rough calculation, the literary works and the potboilers were both outnumbered by the textbooks, many dauntingly technical and in European languages, some seemingly too old to be authoritative sources of the scientific knowledge they sought to impart. One vendor assured me that they sold well, no doubt because new books were either unavailable or unaffordable or both. And in disciplines where the opportunities for experiment, for practical work, and for international exchange were dwindling or have disappeared altogether, textbooks, however old, are all that a student can fall back upon.

Many in the street were, however, just looking. I spotted a young man, I guessed in his early twenties, picking up a book at which he had been gazing intently for some time. He held it, opened the cover, put it down again, then stood there looking at it, unable to walk away. Racked by hesitation, he picked it up once more, studying its contents as if weighing them against alternatives in his mind. Then he asked the vendor the price. When he heard the answer he had a hand in his pocket, perhaps fingering banknotes within; but I saw him shake his head sadly, put the book gently down and walk slowly away. I asked an Arabic-speaking colleague what the book cost. "Five hundred dinars," was the answer. Thirty-three U.S. cents at the prevailing black market rate of exchange, but a week's rations, perhaps, in a country where the typical middle-class wage was four thousand dinars a month.

"For every student like that, you'll also find a fat cat buying books by the armload to cash in on the bargains," a diplomat who knows Iraq well later told me. "The book souk isn't kept alive by foreigners. There aren't enough of us here to do that. Iraqis are still doing most of the buying. But what's sad is that those who love books are mainly doing the selling."

With the book souk at Al Mutanabi still on my mind, I took a trip to see the riverside statue of Scheherazade, the storyteller of the *Arabian Nights*. Only in Baghdad, said friends who know the Arab world, would there be such a statue at all — of a woman, and a woman, at that, renowned for decidedly un-Islamic reasons.

Scheherazade stood twenty feet high in black stone, hands extended, weaving her storytelling spell to an equally immense sculpture of Sultan Shahryar, reclining entranced at a safe distance. Her eyes were large, her gown flowing, her expression modest; but there was no doubt that she dominated the scene, a woman harnessing the power of fiction to her own salvation.

I walked slowly around the plinth on which the pair had been erected and failed to find a plaque or even a date. Nor was there any other visitor or attendant to ask. The site was deserted, and the park in which the statuary stood was overgrown and ill-tended. The city of the fabled Caliph Haroun al-Rasheed, patron of the arts, was now neglecting its own stories — as if, with harsh reality pressing down upon it, even literary Baghdad could no longer seek solace in the magic of myth.

# 39

# Globalization and the
# Human Imagination

*(Speech delivered at the International Festival of
Literature, Berlin, September 10, 2003)*

WHEN THE ORGANIZERS of the International Festival of
Literature first invited me to deliver this lecture, they
suggested something that might reconcile my two worlds —
the UN and literature. In conceiving my topic for today, I
thought about the issues that have dominated my UN life of
late: the forces of globalization, transforming the world irre-
sistibly; the nature of the international mass media, which I
try to influence as a UN official; and the changes that the age
of terrorism, or "9/11," as it is known in America, has wrought
in us, once its shadow has fallen across all our minds and
seized our imaginations. Globalization, the media, our imagination — one could well ask: In the world after 9/11, is
there such a thing as a global imagination?

In other words, I wondered: Has globalization, which has brought McDonald's and Microsoft to every land, brought Mickey Mouse and Nintendo, and for that matter Osama bin Laden and "Chemical Ali," to every mind? With the speed of satellite and cable TV, this is a serious question. The media bring to our breakfast tables and our living rooms, and increasingly to our computers and our mobile phones, glimpses of events from every corner of the globe. Any doubt I might have had about the reach and influence of global mass communications was dispelled when I happened to be in St. Petersburg, Russia, for a conference and was approached by a Tibetan Buddhist monk in his robes, thumping a cymbal and chanting his mantras, who paused in his chanting to say: "I've seen you on BBC!" New communications technology has shrunk the world, and in a real sense made it all one.

And at the risk of being facetious, our major news stories reek of globalization. Take, for instance, an item circulating on the Internet about the death of Princess Diana. An English princess with a Welsh title leaves a French hotel with her Egyptian companion, who has supplanted a Pakistani; she is driven in a German car with a Dutch engine by a Belgian chauffeur full of Scottish whisky; they are chased by Italian paparazzi on Japanese motorcycles into a Swiss-built tunnel and crash; a rescue is attempted by an American doctor using Brazilian medicines; and the story is being told to you now by an Indian visiting Berlin. There's globalization.

But on September 11, 2001, a different challenge arose to the notion of a global imagination. On 9/11, as the Americans have taught us to call it, the twenty-first century was born. If, as the historian Eric Hobsbawm has suggested, the twentieth century really began with the assassination in Sarajevo that sparked World War I, it is fair to suggest that, in the impact it has already had on the shape of our era, the twenty-first century began with the demolition of the World Trade Center just one day short of two years ago.

What do I mean by that? The destruction of the World Trade Center struck a blow not only at the institutions of American and global capitalism but at the self-confidence that undergirded them, the self-confidence of a social and political system that, without needing to think about it too much, believed it had found the answer to life's challenges and could conquer them all. And of course the outrage of September 11 and the anthrax scare that followed it brought the stark consciousness of physical vulnerability to a land that, despite fighting a dozen major wars in its history, has not been directly attacked in living memory. This was the country in which a scholar could complacently propound "the end of history"; now history, like Mark Twain, has proclaimed that reports of its demise were exaggerated. In today's ever-smaller world, geography too offers no protection. If only by bringing home to Americans the end of their insulation from the passions that bedevil the rest of the globe, September 11 changed the world forever.

But the horrifying events of that one day are emblematic of our new century in another crucial way. The defining features of today's world are the relentless forces of globalization, the ease of communications and travel, the shrinking of boundaries, the flow of people of all nationalities and colors across the world, the swift pulsing of financial transactions with the press of a button. The plane, the cell phone, the computer, are the tools of our time. These very forces, which in a more benign moment might have been seen as helping drive the world toward progress and prosperity, were the forces used by the terrorists in their macabre dance of death and destruction. They crossed frontiers easily, coordinated their efforts with technological precision, hijacked jets and crashed them into their targets as their doomed victims made last-minute calls on their cell phones to their loved ones. This was a twenty-first-century crime, and it has defined the dangers and the potential of our time as nothing else can.

It has also provoked a reaction in the United States that will, in turn, leave an indelible mark on the new century. The twentieth century was famously dubbed, by *Time* magazine's Henry Luce, "the American century," but the twenty-first begins with the United States in a state of global economic, political, cultural, and military dominance far greater than any world power has ever before enjoyed. The United States enjoys a level of comparative military power unprecedented in human history; even the Roman Empire at its peak did not come close to outstripping the military capacities of the rest of the world to the extent that the United States does today. But that is not all. When the former French foreign minister, Hubert Vedrine, called the United States a "hyperpower" *(hyperpuissance)*, he was alluding not only to American military dominance but also to the United States as the home of Boeing and Intel, Microsoft and MTV, Hollywood and Disneyland, McDonald's and Kodak — in short, of most of the major products that dominate daily life around our globe.

And yet — before 9/11, Washington had been curiously

ambivalent about its exercise of that dominance, with many influential figures speaking and acting as if the rest of the planet was irrelevant to America's existence or to its fabled pursuit of happiness. After September 11, I was not alone in thinking that there would be no easy retreat into isolationism, no comfort in the illusion that the problems of the rest of the world need not trouble the United States. I found myself on CNN the night after, expressing the outrage and solidarity of those of us working at the United Nations, and I found myself saying not just that "we are all New Yorkers now" — a sentiment many have echoed — but something else: that Americans now understand viscerally the old cliché of the global village. Because 9/11 made it clear that a fire that starts in a remote thatched hut or dusty tent in one corner of that village can melt the steel girders of the tallest skyscrapers at the other end of our global village.

From this observation I went on to suggest in an op-ed in the *International Herald Tribune* that the twenty-first century will be the century of "one world" as never before, with a consciousness that the tragedies of our time are all global in origin and reach, and that tackling them is also a global responsibility that must be assumed by us all. Interdependence, I argued, is now the watchword. Today, two years later, I wonder if I wasn't wrong. One of my favorite stories about the UN Security Council is one about the American diplomat and the French diplomat arguing about a practical problem. "I know how we can solve this," says the American; "We can do this and this and this, and we can solve it." The Frenchman responds, "Yes, yes, yes, that will work in practice. But will it work in theory?" Interdependence is a reality in practice in our globalizing world; but in theory, how can there be genuine interdependence when one country believes it needs everybody else that much less than everybody else needs it? But I am not rushing to disavow my earlier faith in international cooperation. Global challenges require global solutions, and few indeed are the situations in which even the *hyperpuissance* can act completely alone. This truism is being confirmed yet again in Iraq, where the United States is discovering that it has a greater capacity to win wars alone than to construct peace alone. The limitations of military strength in nation-building are readily apparent; as Talleyrand pointed out, the one thing you cannot do with a bayonet is sit on it. Equally important, though, is the need for legitimacy. Acting in the name of international law, and especially through the United Nations, is always preferable to acting in the name of national security, since everyone has a stake in the former. So multilateralism still has a future in Washington.

All the more so because the age of terror is a multilateral threat. The terrorist attack of 9/11 was an assault not just on one country but, in its callous indifference to the lives of innocents from eighty countries around the world, an assault on the very bonds of humanity that tie us all together. To respond to it effectively, we must be united. Terrorism does not originate in one country, its practitioners are not based in one country, its victims are not found in one country — and the response to it must also involve all countries.

Terrorism emerges from blind hatred of an Other, and that in turn is the product of three factors: fear, rage, and incomprehension. Fear of what the Other might do to you, rage at what you believe the Other has done to you, and incomprehension about who or what the Other really is — these three elements fuse together in igniting the deadly combustion that kills and destroys people whose only sin is that they feel none of these things themselves. If terrorism is to be tackled and ended, we will have to deal with each of these three factors by attacking the ignorance that sustains them. We will have to know each other better, learn to see ourselves as others see us, learn to recognize hatred and deal with its causes, learn to dispel fear, and above all just learn about each other.

This is no small challenge. When the United Nations helped reconstruct East Timor after the devastation that accompanied the Indonesian withdrawal, we had to rebuild an entire society, and that meant, in some cases, creating institutions that had never existed before. One of them was a judicial system of international standards, which in practice meant Western standards, complete with the adversarial system of justice in which a prosecutor and a defense attorney attempt to demolish each other's arguments in the pursuit of truth. The UN experts had to train the Timorese in this system. But they discovered that there was one flaw. In Timorese culture, the expected practice is for the accused to confess his crimes, and justice to be meted out compassionately. In order to promote the culture of the "not guilty" plea required by Western court systems, the UN experts had to train the Timorese to lie. Their mental processes — their imaginations — had now truly been globalized.

This brings me to the second half of my argument today. In one sense, the terrorists of 9/11 were attacking the globalization of the human imagination — the godless, materialist, promiscuous culture of the dominant West, embodied in a globalization from which people like them felt excluded. Certainly those who celebrated their act did so from a sense of exclusion. If we speak of the human imagination today, we need to ask what leads surprisingly large numbers of young people to follow the desperate course set for them by fanatics and ideologues. A sense of oppression, of exclusion, of marginalization, can give rise to extremism. Forty years ago, in 1962, the now all-but-forgotten UN secretary general U Thant warned that an explosion of violence could occur as a result of the sense of injustice felt by those living in poverty and despair in a world of plenty. Some 2,600 people died in the World Trade Center on 9/11. But some 26,000 people also died on 9/11, around the world — from starvation, unclean water, and preventable disease. We cannot afford to exclude them from our global imagination.

But that is, of course, not all. If a state cannot even offer its people hope for a better life for their children — by providing access to basic education — then how can we expect those people or those children to resist the blandishments of terror? It should come as no surprise that the Taliban recruited its foot soldiers from the religious schools or madrassas that were the only source of nurture and "education" for many children who had no other source of knowledge available to them; who learned not science or mathematics or computer programming at these schools, but rather only the creed of the Koran and the Kalashnikov — the Koran crudely interpreted, the Kalashnikov crudely made. Their imaginations were, as a result, anything but global.

Which brings me back to the question I raised at the

beginning: Have we fallen into the dangerous illusion that the human imagination can be globalized? In considering an answer, we have to look at the global mass media. The mass media reflects principally the interests of its producers. What passes for international culture is usually the culture of the economically developed world. It's your imagination that is being globalized. American movies and television shows, in particular, can be found on the screens of most countries.

Who else makes the cut to enter the global imagination in our brave new world? Yes, there is the occasional Third World voice, but it speaks a First World language. As far back as the first Congo civil war of 1962, the journalist Edward Behr saw a TV newsman in a camp of violated Belgian nuns calling out, "Anyone here been raped and speak English?" In other words, it was not enough to have suffered: one must have suffered and be able to express one's suffering in the language of the journalist. Which leads to the obvious corollary question: Are those speaking for their cultures in the globalized media the most authentic representatives of them?

Can the Internet compensate? Is it a democratizing tool? In the West, perhaps it has become one, since information is now far more widely accessible to anyone anywhere. But that is not yet true in the developing world. The stark reality of the Internet today is the digital divide: you can tell the rich from the poor by their Internet connections. The gap between the technological haves and have-nots is widening, both between countries and within them. The information revolution, unlike the French Revolution, is a revolution with a lot of *liberté*, some *fraternité*, and no *egalité*.

So the poverty line is not the only line about which we have to think; there is also the high-speed digital line, the fiber optic line — all the lines that exclude those who are literally not plugged in to the possibilities of our brave new world. The key to the Internet divide is the computer keyboard. Those who do not have one risk marginalization; their imagination does not cross borders.

These concerns are real. If they are addressed, if the case for overcoming them is absorbed and applied, the twenty-first century could yet become a time of mutual understanding such as we have never seen before. A world in which it is easier than ever before to meet strangers must also become a world in which it is easier than ever before to see strangers as no different from ourselves.

Ignorance and prejudice are the handmaidens of propaganda, and in most modern conflicts, the men of war prey on the ignorance of the populace to instill fears and arouse hatreds. That was the case in Bosnia and in Rwanda, where murderous, even genocidal ideologies took root in the absence of truthful information and honest education. If only half the effort had gone into teaching those peoples what unites them, and not what divides them, unspeakable crimes could have been prevented.

Freedom of speech also guarantees diversity. As an Indian writer, I have argued that my country's recent experience with the global reach of Western consumer products demonstrates that we can drink Coca-Cola without becoming coca-colonized. India's own popular culture is also part of globalization — the products of Bollywood are exported to expatriate Indian communities abroad. The success of Indian films and music in England and the United States proves that the Empire can strike back.

And it's not just India. A recent study has established that local television programming has begun to overtake made-in-America shows in more and more countries. And as the globalizing world changes, it does not do so only in one direction. In England today, Indian curry houses employ more people than the iron and steel, coal and shipbuilding, industries combined.

In my first novel, *The Great Indian Novel,* I reinvented a two-thousand-year-old epic, the Mahabharata, as a satirical retelling of the story of twentieth-century India, from the British days to the present. My motivation was a conscious one. Most developing countries are also formerly colonized countries, and one of the realities of colonialism is that it appropriates the cultural definition of its subject peoples. Writing about India in English, I cannot but be aware of those who have done the same before me, others with a greater claim to the language but a lesser claim to the land. Think of India in the English-speaking world even today, and you think in images conditioned by Rudyard Kipling and E. M. Forster, by the Bengal Lancers and *The Jewel in the Crown.* But their stories are not my stories, their heroes are not mine; and my fiction seeks to reclaim my country's heritage for itself, to tell, in an Indian voice, a story of India. Let me stress, *a* story of India; for there are always other stories, and other Indians to tell them.

How important is such a literary reassertion in the face

of the enormous challenges confronting a country like India? Can literature matter in a land of poverty, suffering, and underdevelopment? I believe it does.

My novel begins with the proposition that India is not, as people keep calling it, an underdeveloped country, but rather, in the context of its history and cultural heritage, a highly developed one in an advanced state of decay. Such sentiments are the privilege of the satirist; but as a novelist, I believe, with Molière, that you have to entertain in order to edify. But edify to what end? What is the responsibility of the creative artist, the writer, in a developing country in our globalizing world? In my own writing I have pointed to one responsibility — to contribute toward, and to help articulate and give expression to, the cultural identity (shifting, variegated, and multiple, in the Indian case) of the postcolonial society, caught up in the throes of globalization. The vast majority of developing countries have emerged recently from the incubus of colonialism; both colonialism and globalization have in many ways fractured and distorted their cultural self-perceptions. Development will not occur without a reassertion of identity: that this is who we are, this is what we are proud of, this is what we want to be. In this process, culture and development are fundamentally linked and interdependent. The task of the writer is to find new ways (and revive old ones) of expressing his culture, just as his society strives, in the midst of globalization, to find new ways of being and becoming.

As a writer committed to Indian pluralism, I see cultural reassertion as a vital part of the enormous challenges confronting a country like India — as vital as economic development. We are all familiar with the notion that "man does not live by bread alone." In India, I would argue that music, dance, art, and the telling of stories are indispensable to our ability to cope with that vital construct we call the human condition. After all, why does man need bread? To survive. But why survive, if it is only to eat more bread? To live is more than just to sustain life — it is to enrich, and be enriched by, life. Our poorest men and women in the developing world feel the throb of imagination on their pulse, for they tell stories to their children under the starlit skies — stories of their land and its heroes, stories of the earth and its mysteries, stories that have gone into making them what they are. And (since my second novel was about Bollywood) they see and hear stories, too, in the flickering lights of the thousands of cinemas in our land, where myth and escapist fantasy intertwine and moral righteousness almost invariably triumphs with the closing credits.

Globalization, its advocates say, is about growth and development. But it cannot just be a set of figures on GNP tables, a subject for economists and businessmen rather than a matter of people. And if people are to develop, it is unthinkable that they would develop without literature, without song, and dance, and music, and myth, without stories about themselves, and in turn, without expressing their views on their present lot and their future hopes. Development implies dynamism; dynamism requires freedom, the freedom to create; creativity requires, quite simply, imagination.

But in speaking of a cultural reassertion of imagination, I do not want to defend a closed construct. I believe Indians will not become any less Indian if, in Mahatma Gandhi's metaphor, we open the doors and windows of our country and let foreign winds blow through our house. For me the winds of globalization must blow both ways. The UNESCO charter memorably tells us that "as war begins in the minds of men, it is in the minds of men that the foundations of peace must be constructed." This is true not just of war and peace but of the entire fabric of human life and society — which must be constructed in the mind. As the acolytes of Osama bin Laden or the young foot soldiers of the Taliban have taught us, the globe will always have more than a single mind. And that is why cultural diversity is so essential in our shrinking globe. For without a multiplicity of cultures, we cannot realize how peoples of other races, religions, or languages share the same dreams, the same hopes. Without a heterogeneous human imagination, we cannot understand the myriad manifestations of the human condition, nor fully appreciate the universality of human aims and aspirations. This is why, as a writer, I would argue that the specificities of literature are the best antidote to the globalization of the imagination.

Not that literature implies a retreat from the globe: rather, it is the mind shaped by literature that understands the world and responds to its needs. Literature teaches us to empathize, to look beyond the obvious and beneath the surface, to bear in mind the smaller picture — of the ordinary human beings who are ultimately the objects of all public policy. And above all, to remember always that there is more than one side to a story, and more than one answer to a question. Those are fairly useful prescriptions for public policy makers in the era of globalization.

In many ways, the fundamental conflict of our times is

the clash between, no, not civilizations, but doctrines — religious and ethnic fundamentalism on the one hand, secular consumerist capitalism on the other. Thanks to globalization, the world is coming together into a single international market just as it is simultaneously being torn apart by civil war and the breakup of nations. The author Benjamin Barber has written of the twin prospects facing humanity as "Jihad versus McWorld" — "Jihad in the name of a hundred narrowly conceived faiths against every kind of interdependence . . . against technology, against pop culture, against integrated markets; against modernity itself" versus a "McWorld" of globalization run rampant, a world of "fast music, fast computers and fast food — with MTV, Macintosh and McDonald's pressing nations into one commercially homogenous theme park." Both Jihad and McWorld, of course, end up by obliterating our most precious possession — our identity.

Every one of us has many identities. Sometimes religion obliges us to deny the truth about our own complexity by obliterating the multiplicity inherent in our identities. Islamic fundamentalism, in particular, does so because it embodies a passion for pure belonging, a yearning intensified by the threatening tidal wave of globalization as well as by the nature of Middle Eastern politics. Of course there is something precious and valuable in a faith that allows a human being to see himself at one with others stretching their hands out toward God around the world. But can we separate religion from identity? Can we dream of a world in which religion has an honored place but where the need for spirituality will be a personal one, no longer associated with the need to belong? If identity can relate principally to citizenship rather than faith, to a land rather than a doctrine, and if that identity is one that can live in harmony with other identities, then we might resist both Jihad and McWorld.

And for that we must promote pluralism. To strike a personal note, my own faith in religious pluralism is a legacy of my upbringing in secular India. Secularism in India did not mean irreligiousness, which even avowedly atheist parties like the Communists or the southern DMK found unpopular among their voters; indeed, in Calcutta's annual Durga Puja, the Communist parties compete with each other to put up the most lavish Puja pandals. Rather, secularism meant, in the Indian tradition, a profusion of religions, none of which was privileged by the state. I remember how, in the Calcutta neighborhood where I lived during my high school years, the wail of the muezzin calling the Islamic faithful to prayer blended with the tinkling bells and the chant of the mantras at the Hindu Shiva temple and the crackling loudspeakers outside the Sikh *gurudwara* reciting verses from the Granth Sahib. And just two minutes down the road stood St. Paul's Cathedral. Students, office workers, government officials, were all free to wear turbans, veils, caps, whatever their religion demanded of them. That is Indian secularism: accept everyone, privilege no one; nothing is exceptional, no one is humiliated. This secularism is under threat from some in India today, but it remains a precious heritage of all Indians.

Pluralism can only be protected by supporting the development of democracy at a local, national, and international level to provide a context for cultural pluralism to thrive. We must encourage a liberal, free-thinking education that opens minds everywhere rather than closes them.

We must take a stance of respect and humility in our approaches to others, strive for inclusiveness rather than marginalization.

When the terrorists of today and tomorrow have been defeated, our world will still be facing, to use Kofi Annan's phrase, innumerable "problems without passports" — problems of the proliferation of weapons of mass destruction, of the degradation of our common environment, of contagious disease and chronic starvation, of human rights and human wrongs, of mass illiteracy and massive displacement. These are problems that no one country, however powerful, can solve alone, and which are unavoidably the shared responsibility of humankind. They cry out for solutions that, like the problems themselves, also cross frontiers.

Today, whether one is from Tübingen or Tallahassee, it is simply not realistic to think only in terms of one's own country. Global forces press in from every conceivable direction; people, goods, and ideas cross borders and cover vast distances with ever greater frequency, speed, and ease. The Internet is emblematic of an era in which what happens in Southeast Asia or Southern Africa — from democratic advances to deforestation to the fight against AIDS — can affect lives in Germany. As has been observed about water pollution, we all live downstream.

Robert Kagan's famous, if fatuous, proposition that Americans are from Mars and Europeans from Venus has gained wide currency lately. If that is so, where are Africans from — Pluto? They might as well inhabit the most remote planet, for all the attention they are paid by either Americans or Europeans. Yet their problems are an affront to our consciences. The tragic confluence of AIDS, poverty, drought, and famine threatens more human lives in Africa than Iraq ever did. Individual countries may prefer not to deal with such problems directly or alone, but they are impossible to ignore. So handling them together internationally is the obvious way of ensuring they are tackled; it is also the only way. Everyone — Americans, Germans, Indians — will be safer in a world improved by the efforts of the United Nations, efforts in which all the world's peoples have a stake and all enjoy the opportunity to participate. And these efforts will be needed long after Iraq has passed from the headlines.

I have perhaps taken too long in tackling the themes I raised at the beginning of this talk. So let me pull my threads together.

In much of the world there exist societies whose richness lies in their soul and not in their soil, whose past may offer more wealth than their present, whose imagination is more valuable than their technology. Recognizing that this might be the case, and affirming that the imagination is as central to humanity's sense of its own worth as the ability to eat and drink and sleep under a roof, is part of the challenge before the world today. The only way to ensure that this challenge is met is to preserve cultural and imaginative freedom in all societies; to guarantee that individual voices find expression, that all ideas and forms of art are enabled to flourish and contend for their place in the sun. We have heard in the past that the world must be made safe for democracy. That goal is increasingly being realized; it is now time for all of us to work to make the world safe for diversity.

There is an old Indian story about Truth. It seems that in ancient times a brash young warrior sought the hand of a beautiful princess. The king, her father, thought the warrior was a bit too cocksure and callow; he told him he could only marry the princess once he had found Truth. So the young warrior set out on a quest for Truth. He went to temples and to monasteries, to mountaintops where sages meditated and to forests where ascetics scourged themselves, but nowhere could he find Truth. Despairing one day and seeking refuge from a thunderstorm, he found himself in a dank, musty cave. There, in the darkness, was an old hag, with warts on her face and matted hair, her skin hanging in folds from her bony limbs, her teeth broken, her breath malodorous. She greeted him; she seemed to know what he was looking for. They talked all night, and with each word she spoke, the warrior realized he had come to the end of his quest. She was Truth. In the morning, when the storm broke, the warrior prepared to return to claim his bride. "Now that I have found Truth," he said, "what shall I tell them at the palace about you?" The wizened old crone smiled. "Tell them," she said, "tell them that I am young and beautiful."

So Truth is not always true; but that does not mean Truth does not exist. The terrorists failed to see their victims as human beings entitled to their own imaginations. They saw only objects, dispensable pawns in their drive for destruction. Our only effective answer to them must be to defiantly assert our own humanity; to say that each one of us, whoever we are and wherever we are, has the right to live, to love, to hope, to dream, and to aspire to a world in which everyone has that right. A world in which the scourge of terrorism is fought, but so also are the scourges of poverty, of famine, of illiteracy, of ill health, of injustice, and of human insecurity. A world, in other words, in which terror will have no chance to flourish. That could be the world of the twenty-first century that has just been born, and it could be the most hopeful legacy of the horror that has given it birth.

Since you have been told I am an Indian writer, let me tell you an Indian story — a tale from our ancient Puranas. It is a typical Indian story of a sage and his disciples. The sage asks his disciples, "When does the night end?" And the disciples say, "At dawn, of course." The sage says, "I know that. But when does the night end and the dawn begin?" The first disciple, who is from the tropical south of India where I come from, replies: "When the first glimmer of light across the sky reveals the palm fronds on the coconut trees swaying in the breeze, that is when the night ends and the dawn begins." The sage says, "No," so the second disciple, who is from the cold north, ventures: "When the first streaks of sunshine make the snow and ice gleam white on the mountaintops of the Himalayas, that is when the night ends and the dawn begins." The sage says, "No, my sons. When two travelers from opposite ends of our land meet and embrace each other as brothers, and when they realize they sleep under the same sky, see the same stars, and dream the same dreams — that is when the night ends and the dawn begins."

There has been a many a terrible night in the century that has just passed; let us preserve the diversity of the human spirit to ensure that we will all have a new dawn in the century that has just begun.

# 40

# The Anxiety of Audience

WHENEVER I AM ASKED (which is more often than I would wish) to speak to a keen literary audience about my writing, I have to confess I approach the task with some diffidence. Writers are supposed to write; we should leave the pontificating to the critics. But once in a while even writers are forced to think about their craft. I was obliged to do so not long ago when I found myself the subject of a long interview which included the somewhat startling question: "Do you think your text belongs to you?"

I suppose it was inevitable that sooner or later a professor of literature would ask me this post-modernist question. It came from a Dr. Ranjan Ghosh of the University of Burdwan, near Calcutta, and faced with his earnest (and impressively theoretical) approach to my work, I had to explain that I not only have never taken a writing course, I didn't even study literature at university. I thought that would be like learning about girls at a medical school. Indeed, my favorite story of the craft of teaching writing is that of the

British instructor who told his students that to ensure commercial success, a story needed to contain religion, aristocracy, sex, and mystery, and be brief. The briefest submission duly came in, three sentences long: "'My God!' exclaimed the Duchess of Argyll. 'I'm pregnant! Who did it?'" Religion, aristocracy, sex, and mystery, all in the right order, and stunningly brief. The instruction couldn't be bettered. The teacher gave up.

Just as well. For writing, to me, is a wholly instinctual activity; it is about expressing your most intimate feelings and thoughts, and that is as much you as the way you breathe. Nor would I want anyone else to tell me how to write: in my writing, I have always seen the telling of the tale as being as important to me as its author as the tale itself. My text belongs to me in the sense that the words I have chosen to employ are the only ones that are authentic to what I have tried to convey. The same story, the same concerns, can obviously be told or expressed by different writers in different ways. "My" way is the way in which my text has chosen to tell itself through me — and in that form it belongs solely to me.

But I have often felt, as a writer, that I am giving expression to something beyond myself — something that emerges from a different realm that I, perhaps unconsciously, tap into in the act of writing. To that degree, the text is both mine and beyond me, an artifact that emerges like a stream from the ocean of stories that I have been privileged to channel to my readers. For that reason I am prepared to accept the notion that my text may contain hidden meanings of which I myself was not conscious in the act of writing. This is certainly true of painters, who may find something emerging from the brushstrokes they have applied on canvas that was not wholly present in their mind when they were wielding the brush. Though text seems more limiting than paint, the principle is essentially the same for all art.

Of course the critic who reads meanings the author did not consciously intend is guilty of a form of subversion, and the author is entitled to argue that his text does not support the critic's analysis. There the onus is on the critic to make his case, and for the fair-minded reader to draw her own conclusions.

My eight books have all, in different ways, been about my personal exploration of India, of the forces that have made and unmade it, of the historical and philosophical traditions that have shaped the Indian identity. While this is explicit in my four books of nonfiction, my fiction has also sought to explore the Indian condition, particularly by looking at the kinds of stories Indians tell about themselves (whether the stories of our epics and of our nationalist struggle, as in *The Great Indian Novel,* or the stories of our popular cinema, in *Show Business,* or the stories of the identities and histories we construct for ourselves, as in *Riot*). In all three novels, though each is very different from the other two, it is true to say that the architecture of the book speaks of an India of multiple stories, multiple perspectives, multiple tellers, multiple truths.

In my book *The Great Indian Novel* I have rather overtly staked a claim for the tasks of my kind of novel: to affirm and enhance an Indian cultural identity, to broaden understanding of the Indian cultural and historical heritage, and to reclaim for Indians the story of India's national experience and its own reassertion of itself, including the triumphs and disappointments of independence. My story was about the kinds of stories a society tells about itself, and in it I have set out to explore what has made India and nearly unmade it, and about the nature of truth, in life as in fiction, in tradition as in history.

My second novel, *Show Business,* also deals with the stories Indian society tells about itself, except that, instead of the older myths, I have seized on the contemporary myths invented by modern Hindi cinema. One is always looking for new creative metaphors to explore the Indian condition, and in a country of widespread illiteracy, where popular film represents the primary vehicle for the transmission of the fictional experience, cinema is a particularly useful vehicle for this exploration. In addition there are some interesting issues that emerge from the subject itself. The social and political relevance of popular cinema in India, for instance, has been dealt with surprisingly little in Indo-Anglian fiction.

The whole process of the manufacture of our modern myths on celluloid is one that I have found fascinating as a creative issue in itself. My concern has been both with the question, "What do these stories reveal about ourselves?" and with a distinct second set of questions: "How are these stories told? What do they mean to those who make them and those who see them? How do they relate to their lives?"

In *Riot,* the exploration of the build-up to, and eruption of, a Hindu-Muslim riot leads me to raise fundamental questions about the nature of truth, the construction of identity, the invention and reclaiming of the past, the uses of history and the various collisions life offers — collisions between cultures, between attitudes to life, between ideologies, between religious communities, and between men and women. Unlike the other two, this is not a satirical novel, and so it involved an important departure for me as a writer.

I once said to an interviewer, "India matters to me, and through my writing, I would like to matter to India." The lines have been quoted back at me a great deal. Perhaps they sound more grandiose than I had intended.

But the issue of national allegiance they claim is real enough. For the task of the writer, if one can say such a thing, is to find new ways (and revive old ones) of expressing his culture, just as his society strives, through development, to find new ways of being and becoming. In turn, the challenge of finding these new ways obliges the novelist to find not only new stories to tell but new ways of telling them.

In *Riot*, for example, I told the story through newspaper clippings, diary entries, interviews, transcripts, journals, scrapbooks, even poems written by the characters — in other words, using a dozen different voices, different stylistic forms, for different fragments of the story. So the structure of the novel served a substantive purpose, in pointing to different perceptions of "truth" and "history" and therefore of the Indian reality. The narrative suggests that omniscience is not possible; the reader is in the hands of a dozen subjective narrators, and feels that "truth" is indeed a word that can be modified by a possessive pronoun. *Riot* is also a book you can read in any order: though ideally you should read it from beginning to end, you can pick it up from any chapter, go back or forward to any other chapter, and you will bring a different level of awareness to the story. In so doing, you would re-create my text as your own.

So much for why I write, what I write, and even, up to a point, how I write. Now as an Indian writer living in New York, I find myself constantly asked a fourth question with which my American *confrères* never have to contend: "But who do you write for?"

In my case, the question is complicated by both geography and language. I live in the United States and write about India; and I do so in English, a language mastered, if the last census is to be believed, by only 2 percent of the Indian population. There is an unspoken accusation implicit in the question: Am I not guilty of the terrible sin of inauthenticity, of writing about my country for foreigners?

This question has, for many years, bedeviled the work of the growing tribe of writers of what used to be called Indo-Anglian fiction and is now termed, more respectfully, Indian Writing in English. This is ironic, because few developments in world literature have been more remarkable than the emergence, over the last two decades, of a new generation of Indian writers in English. Beginning in 1981 with Salman Rushdie's *Midnight's Children*, they have expanded the boundaries of their craft and of their nation's literary heritage, enriching English with the rhythms of ancient legends and the larger-than-life complexities of another civilization, while reinventing India in the confident cadences of English prose. Of the many unintended consequences of Empire, it is hard to imagine one of greater value to both colonizers and colonized.

The new Indian writers dip into a deep well of memory

and experience far removed from those of their fellow novelists in the English language. But whereas Americans or Englishmen or Australians have also set their fictions in distant lands, Indians write of India without exoticism, their insights undimmed by the dislocations of foreignness. And they do so in an English they have both learned and lived, an English of freshness and vigor, a language that is as natural to them as their quarrels at the school playground or the surreptitious notes they slipped each other in their classrooms.

Yet Indian critics still suggest that there is something artificial and un-Indian about an Indian writing in English. One critic disparagingly declared that the acid test ought to be, "Could this have been written only by an Indian?" I have never been much of a literary theoretician, but for most, though not all, of my own writing, I would answer that my works could not only have been written only by an Indian, but only by an Indian in English.

I write for anyone who will read me, but first of all for Indians like myself, Indians who have grown up speaking, writing, playing, wooing, and quarreling in English, all over India. (Few writers really choose a language: the circumstances of their upbringing ensure that the language chooses them.) Members of this class have entered the groves of academe and condemned themselves in terms of bitter self-reproach: one Indian scholar, Harish Trivedi, has asserted (in English) that Indian writers in that language are "cut off from the experiential mainstream, and from that common cultural matrix . . . shared with writers of all other Indian languages." Trivedi metaphorically cites the fictional English-medium school in an R. K. Narayan story whose students must first rub off the sandalwood-paste caste-marks from their foreheads before they enter its portals: "For this golden gate is only for the *déraciné* to pass through, for those who have erased their antecedents."

It's an evocative image, even though I thought the secular Indian state was *supposed* to encourage the erasure of casteism from the classroom. But the more important point is that writers like myself do share a "common cultural matrix," albeit one devoid of helpfully identifying caste-marks. It is one that consists of an urban upbringing and a pan-national outlook on the Indian reality. I do not think this is any less authentically "Indian" than the worldviews of writers in other Indian languages. Why should the rural peasant or the small-town schoolteacher with his sandalwood-smeared forehead be considered more quintessentially Indian than the punning collegian or the Bombay socialite, who are as much a part of the Indian reality?

India is a vast and complex country; in Whitman's phrase, it contains multitudes. I write of an India of multiple truths and multiple realities, an India that is greater than the sum of its parts. English expresses that diversity better than any Indian language precisely because it is not rooted in any one region of my vast country. At the same time, as an Indian, I remain conscious of, and connected to, my pre-urban and non-Anglophone antecedents: my novels reflect an intellectual heritage that embraces the ancient epic the Mahabharata, the Kerala folk dance called the *ottamthullal* (of which my father was a gifted practitioner), and the Hindi B movies of Bollywood, as well as Shakespeare, Wodehouse, and the Beatles.

As a first-generation urbanite myself, I keep returning to the Kerala villages of my parents, in my life as in my writing. Yet I have grown up in Bombay, Calcutta, and Delhi, Indian cities a thousand miles apart from each other; the mother of my children is half-Kashmiri, half-Bengali; and my own mother now lives in the southern town of Coimbatore. This may be a wider cultural matrix than the good Dr. Trivedi imagined, but it draws from a rather broad range of Indian experience. And English is the language that brings those various threads of my India together, the language in which my former wife could speak to her mother-in-law, the language that enables a Calcuttan to function in Coimbatore, the language that serves to express the complexity of that polyphonous Indian experience better than any other language I know. As a novelist, I believe in distracting in order to instruct — I subscribe to Molière's credo, "Le devoir de la comédie est de corriger les hommes en les divertissant." You have to educate people while diverting them.

It is true that, to some degree, my novels are didactic ones masquerading as entertainments. I like my readers to work a little for their pleasure, but the pleasure is intended to transcend the work. As for my audience, I have to admit that the entertainment and the education might strike different readers differently. *The Great Indian Novel,* as a satirical reinvention of the Mahabharata, inevitably touches Indians in a way that most foreigners will not fully appreciate, but my publishers in the West enjoyed its stories and the risks it took with narrative form. *Show Business* did extremely well with American reviewers and readers, who enjoyed the way I tried to portray the lives and stories of

Bollywood as a metaphor for Indian society. With *India: From Midnight to the Millennium*, an attempt to look back at the last fifty years of India's history, I found an additional audience of Indian-Americans seeking to rediscover their roots; their interest has helped the American edition outsell the Indian one. In *Riot*, for the first time, I had major non-Indian characters, Americans as it happens, and that was bound to influence the way the book was perceived both in America and in India. Inevitably the English language fundamentally affects the content of each book, but it does not determine the audience of the writer; as long as translations exist, language is a vehicle, not a destination.

Of course, there is no shame in acknowledging that English is a legacy of the colonial connection, but one no less useful and valid than the railways, the telegraphs, or the law courts that were also left behind by the British. Historically, English helped us find our Indian voice: that great Indian nationalist Jawaharlal Nehru wrote his *Discovery of India* in English. But the eclipse of that dreadful phrase "the Indo-Anglian novel" has occurred precisely because Indian writers have evolved well beyond the British connection to their native land. The days when Indians wrote novels in English either to flatter or rail against their colonial masters are well behind us. Now we have Indians in India writing as naturally about themselves in English as Australians or South Africans do, and their tribe has been supplemented by India's rich diaspora in the United States, which has already produced a distinctive crop of impressive novelists, with Pulitzer Prizes and National Book Awards to their names.

Their addresses don't matter, because writers really live inside their heads and on the page, and geography is merely a circumstance. They write secure of themselves in their heritage of diversity, and they write free of the anxiety of audience, for theirs are narratives that appeal as easily to Americans as to Indians — and indeed to readers irrespective of ethnicity.

Surely that's the whole point about literature — that for a body of fiction to constitute a literature it must rise above its origins, its setting, even its language, to render accessible to a reader anywhere some insight into the human condition. Read my books and those of other Indian writers not because we're Indian, not necessarily because you are interested in India, but because they are worth reading in and of themselves. And each time you pick up one of my books, ask not for whom I write: I write for you.

So — to go back to the question with which we began — does my text belong to me? I write, as George Bernard Shaw said, for the same reason a cow gives milk: it's inside me, it's got to come out, and in a real sense I would suffer if I couldn't. It's the way I express my reaction to the world I live in, see around me, and try to imagine. It would be as futile to claim ownership of it as for a cow to assert she owns the milk she has provided. No, dear reader, the text no longer belongs to me. It belongs to you.